THE FAMILY
Handyman

101 SATURDAY MORNING
PROJECTS

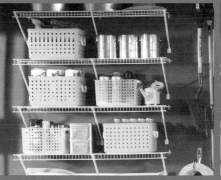

ORGANIZE   **DECORATE**   **REJUVENATE**

Reader's Digest

The Reader's Digest Association, Inc.
New York, NY/Montreal

A READER'S DIGEST BOOK

Copyright © 2010 The Reader's Digest Association, Inc.

All rights reserved. Unauthorized reproduction, in any manner, is prohibited.

Reader's Digest is a registered trademark of The Reader's Digest Association, Inc.

The Family Handyman is a registered trademark of RD Publications, Inc.

FOR THE FAMILY HANDYMAN
Editor in Chief: Ken Collier
Associate Editor: Mary Flanagan
Design Director: Sara Koehler
Administrative Manager: Alice Garrett
Lead Designer: Bob Ungar
Page Layout: Bruce Bonenstingl, Theresa Marrone
Production Manager: Judy Rodriguez

FOR READER'S DIGEST
U.S. Project Editor: Kim Casey
Editorial Assistance: Lauren Hanson
Project Production Coordinator: Wayne Morrison
Senior Art Director: George McKeon
Executive Editor, Trade Publishing: Dolores York
Manufacturing Manager: Elizabeth Dinda
Associate Publisher: Rosanne McManus
President and Publisher, Trade Publishing: Harold Clarke

Library of Congress Cataloging-in-Publication Data

101 Saturday morning projects : organize, decorate, rejuvenate.
　　p. cm.
　ISBN 978-1-60652-189-2 (hardcover)
　ISBN 978-1-60652-018-5 (paperback)
1. Dwellings--Maintenance and repair--Amateurs' manuals. 2. Dwellings---Remodeling--Amateurs' manuals. 3. Storage in the home--Amateurs' manuals. 4. Do-it-yourself work. I. Reader's Digest Association. II. Title: One hundred and one Saturday morning projects. III. Title: Saturday morning projects.
　TH4817.3.A19 2010
　643'.7--dc22
　　　　　　　　　2009038049

Text, photography, and illustrations are based on articles previously run in *The Family Handyman*, 2915 Commers Dr., Suite 700, Eagan, MN 55121.

We are committed to both the quality of our products and the service we provide to our customers. We value your comments, so please feel free to contact us.

　　　　The Reader's Digest Association, Inc.
　　　　Adult Trade Publishing
　　　　44 S. Broadway
　　　　White Plains, NY 10601

For more Reader's Digest products and information, visit our website:
　　　　www.rd.com (in the United States)

Printed in China

1 3 5 7 9 10 8 6 4 2 (hardcover)
7 9 10 8 6 (paperback)

Contents

This chapter is loaded with easy-to-build projects that will enhance your home. You'll find projects for increasing kitchen and bathroom storage, organizing the house, adding attractive shelving, and building basic, yet fully functional, pieces of furniture.

Chapter 1

projects

1 Glass shelves
for bathroom storage

Most bathrooms have one space you can count on for additional storage, and that's over the toilet. Open glass shelving is a great place to display decorative bathroom bottles or knickknacks. There are zillions of glass shelving systems on the market. Follow the directions that come with the system for the installation details, but read on for help anchoring them to the wall, because you probably won't have studs exactly where you need them. Here, masking tape is used to avoid marking the walls.

1 Apply a strip of 2-in.-wide masking tape above the center of the toilet and on both sides where the shelf brackets will be mounted. Draw a center line with a level and mark the heights of the shelves on the center tape. Transfer the heights to the bracket tape with a 2-ft. level. Then measure from the center line to mark the exact left and right locations for the brackets.

Open glass shelving is a great place to display decorative bathroom bottles or knickknacks.

tip Use self-drilling metal wall anchors to support the brackets. The anchors are easy to install and you don't have to worry about finding a stud—the anchors attach to the drywall. You can remove the shelves and brackets to paint the wall, and the anchors will stay in place, ready for reuse.

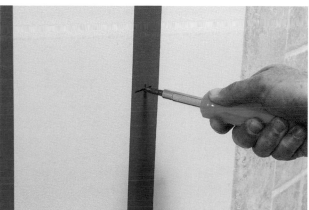

2 Indent the drywall at the marks with a Phillips head screwdriver and remove the tape.

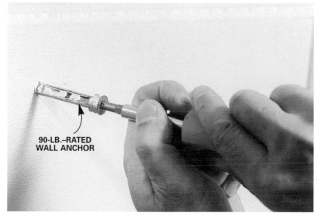

90-LB.–RATED WALL ANCHOR

3 Drive hollow wall anchors through the drywall.

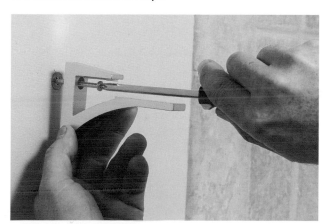

4 Screw the brackets to the wall using the screws included with the anchors.

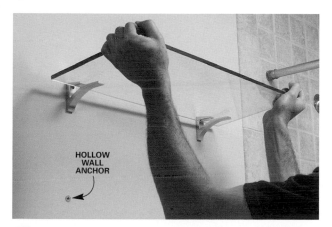

HOLLOW WALL ANCHOR

5 Center the shelves between the brackets, then press firmly into place.

2 **Heavy-duty** storage shelves

 Store-bought shelving units are either hard to assemble and flimsy or awfully expensive. Here's a better solution. These shelves are strong and easy to build and cost about $70. This sturdy shelf unit is sized to hold standard bankers' boxes ($4 each). If you want deeper storage, build the shelves 24 in. deep and buy 24-in.-deep boxes. If you prefer to use plastic storage bins, measure the size of the containers and modify the shelf and upright spacing to fit.

Refer to the dimensions below to mark the location of the horizontal 2x2 on the back of four 2x4s. Also mark the position of the 2x4 uprights on the 2x2s. Then simply line up the marks and screw the 2x2s to the 2x4s with pairs of 2-1/2-in. wood screws. Be sure to keep the 2x2s and 2x4s at right angles. Rip two 4 x 8-ft. sheets of 1/2-in. MDF (medium-density fiberboard), plywood or OSB (oriented-strand board) into 16-in.-wide strips and screw it to the 2x2s to connect the two frames and form the shelving unit.

Build sturdy, simple shelves, custom-sized to hold boxes or other storage containers.

> ✳ **tip** **Labeling plastic bins**
> If you choose plastic bins rather than cardboard bankers' boxes, label the plastic with a wet-erase marker. When it's time to relabel the bin, just wipe away the marks with a damp rag.

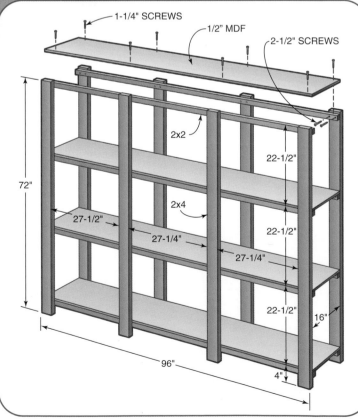

3 Stud-space cabinet

When you can't find a convenient nook for a set of shelves, you can often create one by recessing the shelves into the wall itself. Choose the location before you build the project to make sure it will fit. Start by looking for a space with no obvious obstructions. Locate the studs with a stud finder. Some stud finders can also locate electrical wires and plumbing pipes inside walls. When you've found a promising spot, cut a 6-in.-square inspection hole between the studs. Use a flashlight and a small mirror to inspect the stud cavity for obstructions. You often can modify the size of the cabinet to avoid obstructions.

When you find a good space, mark the perimeter of the opening and use a drywall keyhole saw to cut it out (for plaster, use a jig saw). Measure the opening and subtract 1/4 in. from the height and width to determine the outer dimensions of your cabinet.

For standard 2x4 stud walls with 1/2-in.-thick drywall, build the cabinet frame from 1x4s that measure 3-1/2 in. wide (see illustration). If your walls are different, adjust the depth of the frame accordingly. Then add a 1/4-in. back. Screw 1/4-in. pegboard to the back so you can hang stuff from pegboard hooks.

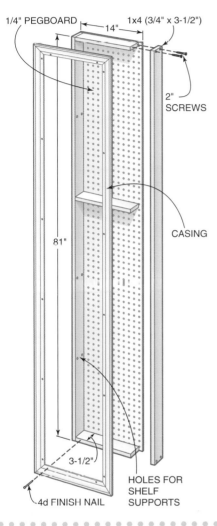

1/4" PEGBOARD

14"

1x4 (3/4" x 3-1/2")

2" SCREWS

81"

CASING

HOLES FOR SHELF SUPPORTS

3-1/2"

4d FINISH NAIL

Remove the drywall from between two studs. Construct a shallow cabinet to fit the space.

Add casing that matches the trim in your house. Drill holes into the sides to accept shelf supports. Shelf supports fit in 3mm, 5mm or 1/4-in. holes depending on the style.

Install the cabinet by slipping it into the opening, leveling it and nailing through the trim into the studs on each side. Use 6d finish nails placed every 12 in. along both sides.

4 Joist-space space saver

Don't waste all that space between joists in a basement or garage. Screw wire shelving to the underside of the joists. An 8-ft. x 16-in. length of wire shelving and a pack of plastic clips (sold separately) costs $21.

Screw a wire closet shelf to the underside of joists to create a shelf that's strong, easy to see through and won't collect dust.

5 Cabinet **rollouts**

Base cabinets have the least convenient storage space in the entire kitchen. To access it, you have to stoop way over or even get down on your knees and then sort through all the stuff in front to find that particular omelet pan or storage container. What a pain. Rollouts solve that problem. They make organizing and accessing your cabinet contents back-friendly and frustration free.

If you're stuck with cabinets without rollouts, don't despair. Here you'll learn how to retrofit nearly any base cabinet with roll-outs that'll work as well as or better than any factory-built units.

It's really very easy. Once you take measurements, you can build the rollout drawer (Photos 2 – 6), its "carrier" (Photos 7 – 9), and attach the drawer slides (Photos 6 and 7), all in your shop. Mounting the unit in the cabinet is simple (Photos 10 – 12). You'll also learn how to construct a special rollout for recycling or trash (Photos 14 – 15).

The project will go faster if you have a table saw and miter saw to cut out all the pieces. A circular saw and cutting guide will

work too; it'll just take a little longer. You can build a pair of rollouts in a Saturday morning for about $20 per shelf.

What wood products to buy

These rollout drawers are made entirely of 1/2-in. Baltic birch plywood. Baltic birch is favored by cabinetmakers because it's "void free," meaning that the thin veneers of the ply-wood core are solid wood. Therefore sanded edges will look smooth and attractive. If your local home center doesn't stock Baltic birch, find it at any hardwood specialty store.

If you choose, you can make the sides of the rollout drawers from any 1x4 solid wood that matches your cabinets and then finish to match (use plywood for the bases). But if you use 3/4-in. material for the sides, subtract 3 in. from the opening to size the rollout (not 2-1/2 in., as described in Photo 2).

The drawer carriers (Figure A) are made from pine 1x4s for the sides (Photo 7) and 1/4-in. MDF (medium-density fiberboard) for the bases (Photo 9). The MDF keeps the drawer base spaced properly while you shim and attach it to the cabinet sides. It can be removed and reused for other carriers after installation. If MDF isn't available, substitute any other 1/4-in. hardboard or plywood.

Side-mounted slides are the best choice among drawer slide options. Their ball-bearing mechanisms and precise fit make for smooth-operating drawers that hold 90 lbs. or more. Shown here are 22-in. full-extension KV (800-253-1561; www.knapeandvogt.com) brand side-mount drawer slides that have a 90-lb. weight rating. That means they'll be sturdy enough even for a drawer full of canned goods. Full-extension slides allow the rollout to extend completely past the cabinet front so you can access all the contents. Expect to pay about $6 to $15 per set of slides at any home center or well-stocked hardware store.

Measure carefully before you build

Nearly all standard base cabinets are 23-1/4 in. deep from the inside of the face frame (Photo 1) to the back of the cabinet. So in most cases, 22-in.-long rollout drawer and carrier sides will clear with room to spare. Check your cabinets to make sure that 22-in. rollouts will work. If you have shallower cabinets, subtract whatever is necessary when you build your rollouts and their carriers (see Figure A).

Then measure the cabinet width. The

FACE FRAME

1 Open the cabinet doors to their widest point and measure the narrowest part of the cabinet opening (usually at the hinges).

Figure A
Standard rollout

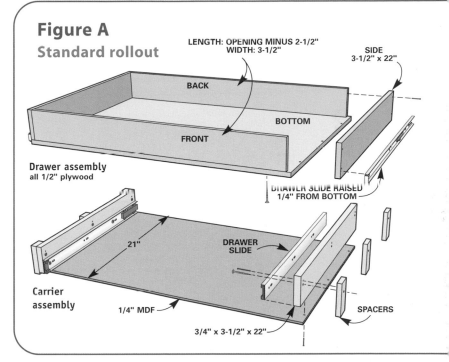

LENGTH: OPENING MINUS 2-1/2"
WIDTH: 3-1/2"

BACK

SIDE 3-1/2" x 22"

BOTTOM

FRONT

Drawer assembly all 1/2" plywood

DRAWER SLIDE RAISED 1/4" FROM BOTTOM

21"

DRAWER SLIDE

Carrier assembly

1/4" MDF

SPACERS

3/4" x 3-1/2" x 22"

Figure B
Wastebasket rollout

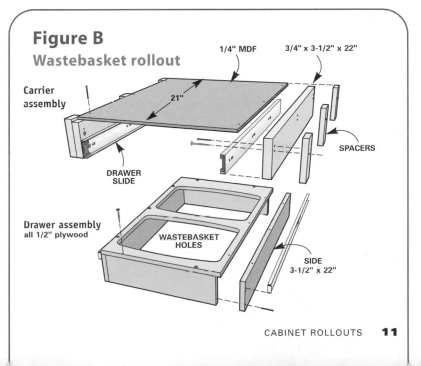

1/4" MDF

3/4" x 3-1/2" x 22"

Carrier assembly

21"

SPACERS

DRAWER SLIDE

Drawer assembly all 1/2" plywood

WASTEBASKET HOLES

SIDE 3-1/2" x 22"

2 Rip 1/2-in. plywood down to 3-1/2 in. wide and cut two 22-in. lengths (drawer sides) and two more to the measured width minus 2-1/2 in. (drawer front and back; Figure A).

3 Clamp or screw two straight 12-in. 2x4s to the corner of a flat surface to use as a squaring jig. Use a carpenter's square to ensure squareness. Leave a 2-in. gap at the corner.

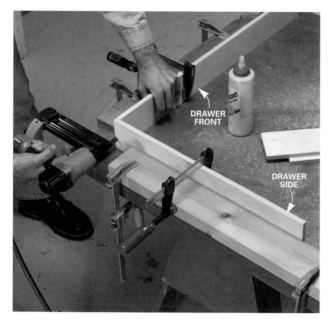

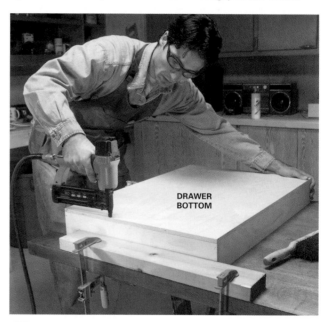

4 Spread wood glue on the ends and clamp a drawer side and front in place, then pin the corner together with three 1-1/4-in. brads. Repeat for the other three corners.

5 Cut a 1/2-in. plywood bottom to size. Apply a thin bead of glue to the bottom edges, and nail one edge of the plywood flush with a side, spacing nails every 4 in. Then push the frame against the jig to square it and nail the other three edges.

drawer has to clear the narrowest part of the opening (Photo 1). When taking this measurement, include hinges that protrude into the opening, the edge of the door attached to the hinges, and even the doors that won't open completely because they hit nearby appliances or other cabinets. Plan on making the drawer front and rear parts 2-1/2 in. shorter than the opening (Figure A).

Shown here are drawers with 3-1/2-in.-high sides, but you can customize your own. Plan on higher sides for lightweight plastic storage containers or other tall or tippy items, and lower sides for stable, heavier items like small appliances.

Drawer slides aren't as confusing as they seem

At first glance, drawer slides are pretty hard to figure out, but

after you install one set, you'll be an expert. They're sold in pairs and each of the pairs has two parts. The "drawer part" attaches to the rollout while the "cabinet part" attaches to the carrier. To separate them for mounting, slide them out to full length and then push, pull or depress a plastic release to separate the two parts. The cabinet part, which always encloses the drawer part, is the larger of the two, and the mounting screw hole locations will be shown in the directions. (Screws are included with the drawer slides.) The oversized holes allow for some adjustment, but if you follow our instructions, you shouldn't have to fuss with fine-tuning later. When mounting the slides, you should make sure to hold them flush with the front of the rollout drawer and carrier sides (Photos 6 and 7). The front of the drawer part usually has a bent metal stop that faces the front of the drawer.

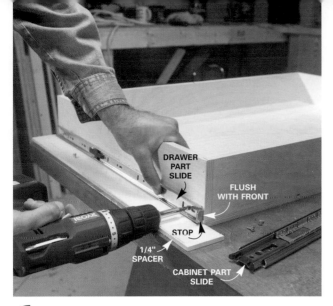

6 Separate the drawer slides and space the drawer part 1/4 in. up from the bottom. Hold it flush to the front and screw it to the rollout side.

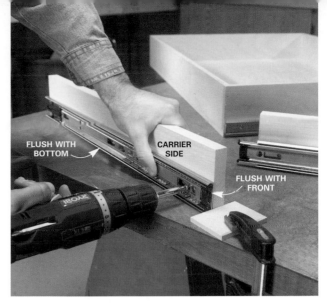

7 Mount the carrier part of the drawer slide flush with the bottom and front of the carrier sides.

8 Slide the drawer and carrier sides together and measure the carrier width. Cut 1/4-in. MDF to that width and 1 in. less than the carrier depth (usually 21 in.).

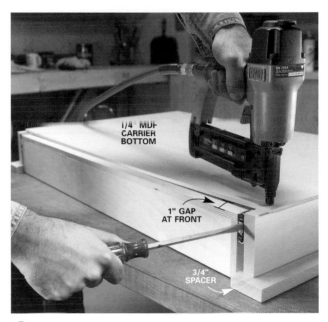

9 Rest the carrier assembly on 3/4-in.-thick spacers, pull the carrier sides slightly away from the drawer, then nail on the carrier bottom (no glue).

Assembling parts and finishing the rollouts

It's important to build the rollout drawers perfectly square for them to operate properly. Photos 3 and 4 show a simple squaring jig that you can clamp to a corner of any workbench to help. Use the jig to nail the frame together, but even more important, to hold the frame square when you nail on the bottom panel. If it hangs over the sides even a little, the drawer slides won't work smoothly.

Use 1-1/4-in. brads for all of the assembly. Glue the drawer parts together but not the bottom of the carrier. It only serves as a temporary spacer for mounting. (After mounting the carrier and drawer, you can remove it if it catches items on underlying drawers or even reuse it for other carriers.) If you'd like to finish

the rollout for a richer look and easier cleaning, sand the edges with 120-grit paper and apply a couple of coats of water-based polyurethane before mounting the slides.

To figure the spacer thickness, rest the lower carrier on the bottom of the shelf, push it against one side of the cabinet and measure the gap on the other (Photo 10). Rip spacers to half that measurement and cut six of them to 3-1/2 in. long. Slip the spacers between both sides of the carrier to check the fit. They should slide in snugly but not tightly. Recut new spacers if needed. In out-of-square cabinets, you may have to custom-cut spacers for each of the three pairs of spacers, so check each of the three spacer positions. It's easiest to tack the spacers to the rollouts to hold them in place before predrilling 1/8-in. holes and running the screws through

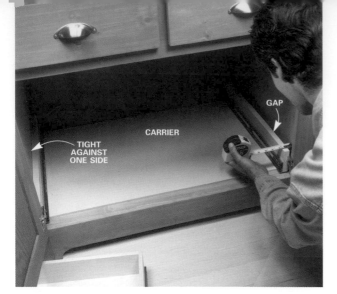

10 Remove the drawer, tip the carrier into the cabinet and push the carrier against one side. Measure the gap and rip six 3-1/2-in.-long spacers to half of the thickness.

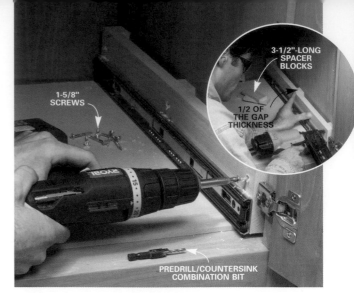

11 Nail the spacers to the center and each end of the carrier sides (not into the cabinet; see inset photo). Then predrill and screw the carrier sides to the cabinet in the center of each shim. Slide the drawer back into place.

12 Cut plywood spacers to temporarily support the upper rollout and set them onto the carrier below. Rest the second carrier on the spacers and install it as shown in Photo 11.

13 Build an upside-down version of the carrier and rollouts for the wastebasket drawer (Figure B). Center and trace around the rim of the wastebasket(s). Use a compass to mark the opening 1/2 in. smaller.

the rollout frames and spacers and into the cabinet sides (Photo 11).

Slip the rollout into its carrier and check for smooth operation. If you followed the process, it should work perfectly. If it binds, it's probably because the spacers are too wide or narrow. Pull out the carrier, remove the spacers and start the spacer process all over again.

The best way to level and fasten the upper rollout is to support it on temporary plywood spacers (Photo 12). The photo shows pieces of plywood cut 7 in. high. In reality, the exact height is up to you. If, for example, you want to store tall boxes of cereal on the bottom rollout and shorter items on the top, space the top rollout higher. You can even build and install three or more rollouts in one cabinet for mega storage of short items like cans, cutlery or beverages. (Those now-obsolete shelves you're replacing with rollouts are good stock to use for your spacers.) Again, pin the spacers in place with a brad or two to hold them while you're predrilling and screwing the carriers to the cabinet sides. Be sure to select screw lengths that won't penetrate exposed cabinet sides! In most cases, 1-5/8-in. screws are the best choice. Strive for 1/2-in. penetration into the cabinet sides. Countersink the heads as far as necessary to get the proper penetration.

Building wastebasket rollouts

Wastebasket rollouts are just upside-down versions of standard rollouts. That is, the carrier is mounted on the top rather than the bottom of the rollout and the slides are positioned at the bottom edge of the carrier sides. That lets the wastebasket lip clear the MDF. Follow Figure B on p. 11 for the details.

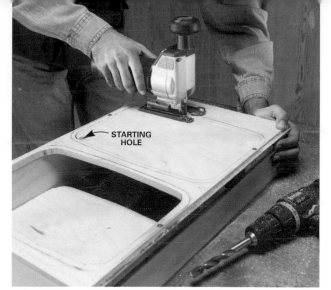

14 Drill 1/2-in. starting holes and cut the openings with a jigsaw.

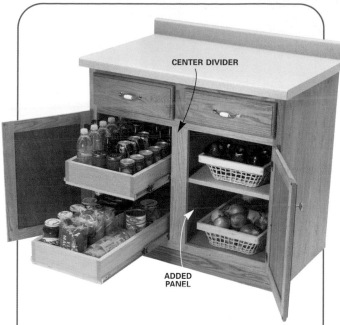

CENTER DIVIDER

ADDED PANEL

15 Mount the wastebasket carrier and drawer as shown in Photos 10 and 11.

This wastebasket rollout is built inside an 18-in.-wide cabinet, so it fits two plastic containers back to back. If you only have a 15-in. cabinet to work with, you may be limited to one container mounted sideways. Buy your containers ahead of time to fit your opening.

With some wastebasket rollouts, you may need to knock the MDF free from the carriers after mounting so the wastebasket lips will clear. That's OK; it won't affect operation.

It may not always work to center rollout assemblies in all openings with equal spacers on each side. That's especially true with narrow single cabinets that only have one pair of hinges. It's best to test things before permanent mounting. But if you make a mistake, it's a simple matter to unscrew the assembly, adjust the shims and remount everything.

Building rollouts in cabinets with center dividers

Many two-door cabinets have a center divider (photo above), which calls for a slightly different strategy. You can still build rollouts, but they'll be narrower versions on each side of the divider. (Check to be sure they won't be so narrow that they're impractical.) The key is to install a 3/4-in. plywood, particleboard or MDF panel between the center divider and the cabinet back to support the carriers.

Cut the panel to fit loosely between the divider and the cabinet back and high enough to support the top rollout position. Center the panel on the back side and middle of the divider and screw it into place with 1-in. angle brackets (they're completely out of sight). Use a carpenter's square to position the panel perfectly centered and vertical on the cabinet back and anchor it there, again using angle brackets. Measure, build and install the rollouts as shown here.

ROLLOUT

1" ANGLE BRACKET

ADDED PANEL

Super-simple bath cabinet

molding is appropriate for this project. For a more contemporary look, you can skip the crown and base altogether since they're purely decorative.

Build a basic box

Cut the plywood parts to size. The dimensions used here are given in the Cutting list (p. 17). To make the short end cuts, use the homemade guide shown in Photo 3 and described below.

Assemble the cabinet box with glue and screws, followed by wood dowels for extra strength (Photo 1). You can buy long dowels and cut them into short pieces, but dowels precut and fluted for woodworking are easier to work with. This assembly method is quick, easy and strong. But because it requires lots of wood filler to hide the fasteners, it's for painted work only. If you want to use stain and a clear finish, biscuits or pocket screws are a better choice.

Drill 1/8-in. pilot and countersink holes for the screws using a drill bit that does both at once ($6 at home centers). Attach the top, bottom and cleats to one side, then add the other side. Mark the middle shelf position on the sides, slip it into place and fasten it (there's no need for glue).

Before you drill the dowel holes, make sure the box is square by taking diagonal measurements; equal measurements mean the box is square. If necessary, screw a strip of plywood diagonally across the back of the box to hold it square. For clean, splinter-free holes, drill the dowel holes with a 3/8-in. brad-point bit ($5), making the holes 1/8 in. deeper than the length of the dowels. That way, you can sink the dowels below the surface of the plywood and fill the holes with wood filler. With the box completed, drill holes for the adjustable shelf supports (Photo 2) using a brad-point drill bit. Most shelf supports require a 1/4-in. hole.

Cut and hang the doors

Cut the doors using a saw guide (Photo 3). To make a guide, screw a straight 1x3 to a 14 x 18-in. scrap of 3/4-in. plywood. Then run your saw along the 1x3 to cut off the excess plywood and create a guide that steers your saw perfectly straight and indicates the exact path of the cut. Simply mark the doors, align the guide with the marks, clamp it in place and cut.

Screw the hinges to the doors 3 in. from the ends (Photo 4). The fronts and backs of louvered doors look similar, so check twice before you drill. Stand the doors against the cabinet, setting them on spacers to create a 1/8-in. gap at the bottom. The gap between the doors should also be about 1/8 in. Clamp each door in position and screw the hinges in place (Photo 5). If the doors don't align perfectly because the box is slightly out-of-square, don't worry. You can square the box when you hang it. The hinges also adjust up or down 1/16 in.

In most bathrooms, a picture or small shelf hangs above the toilet. But you can make better use of that space with an attractive cabinet that offers about three times as much storage as a typical medicine cabinet.

This article will show you how to build it. The simple joinery and store-bought doors make this a great project for the woodworking novice. Assembling the crown and base is a bit trickier, but this article shows that process, too.

The total materials bill for this cabinet was $140. You'll need a miter saw to cut the trim. A table saw and a brad nailer will save time, but you can make all the cuts with a circular saw and drive the nails by hand if you prefer.

The height and width of your cabinet may differ slightly from this one, depending on the bifold doors available at your home center. So choose your doors first and then alter the lengths of the sides, top, bottom and middle shelves if necessary. Bifold closet doors are sold as a pair, usually joined by hinges. Each of the doors shown here measured 11-15/16 in. wide, and were cut to length as shown in the photo in the sidebar on p. 18.

The easy-to-install hinges used here are available online (see Materials list, p. 17). All the other tools and materials, including the cabinet doors, are available at home centers. You may not find the exact same crown and base moldings used here, but most home centers carry a similar profile. Any 2-1/4-in. crown

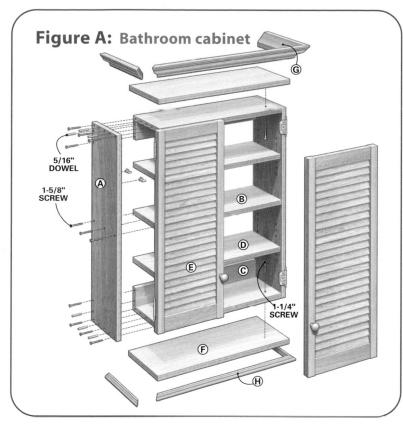

Figure A: Bathroom cabinet

5/16" DOWEL

1-5/8" SCREW

(A)
(B)
(C)
(D)
(E)
(F)
(G)
(H)

1-1/4" SCREW

1-1/4" SCREW

Materials list

Item	Qty.
4' x 8' x 3/4" birch plywood	1
2-1/4"-wide crown molding	5'
3/4"-tall base cap molding	5'
1-1/4" screws	1 box
1-5/8" screws	1 box
5/16" or 3/8" dowels	16
1-1/2" finish nails	1 box
Hinges*	4
Shelf supports	8
Spray primer	1 can
Spray paint	2 cans
Wood glue	
Wood filler	

*To order hinges, call (800) 383-0130 or go to www.wwhardware.com. This project uses No. A03180TB-G9. For other styles and finishes, do a search for "a03180".

1 Assemble the cabinet box quickly with glue and wood screws. Then add glued dowels for rock-solid joints. Drill splinter-free dowel holes with a brad-point bit.

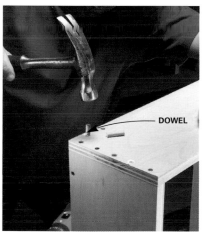

DOWEL

BRAD-POINT BIT

Cutting list

Key	Qty.	Size & Description
A	2	8" x 32-5/8" sides
B	3	8" x 22-1/2" top, bottom and middle shelf
C	2	3" x 22-1/2" top and bottom cleats
D	2	8" x 22-1/4" adjustable shelves
E	2	11-15/16" x 32-3/8" doors
F	2	9" x 24" crown and base frames
G	3	2-1/4"-wide crown molding (cut to fit)
H	3	3/4"-tall base molding (cut to fit)

Except for moldings, all parts are 3/4-in. plywood.

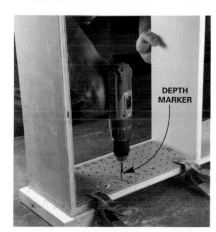

DEPTH MARKER

2 Drill shelf support holes using a scrap of pegboard to position the holes. Wrap masking tape around the drill bit so you don't drill all the way through.

SAW GUIDE

CLOSET DOOR

3 Cut the doors using a homemade saw guide to ensure a straight cut. Lay the door face down so any splintering takes place on the back of the door.

SELF-CENTERING BIT

4 Mount the hinges on the doors. A self-centering drill bit positions the screw holes for perfectly placed hinges.

5 Position the doors carefully and clamp them to the cabinet. Then screw the hinges to the cabinet from inside for a foolproof, exact fit.

HOLD-DOWN BLOCK

6 Cut the crown molding upside down and leaning against the fence. Clamp a block to the saw's fence so you can hold the molding firmly against the fence.

7 Nail the crown to the frame. Nail the mitered corners only if necessary. If they fit tight and are perfectly aligned, let the glue alone hold them together.

CROWN

BASE

8 Center the crown on the cabinet and fasten it with screws driven from inside. Then center the cabinet on the base and attach it the same way.

Add the crown and base

Measure the top of the cabinet (including the doors) and cut the plywood crown and base frames to that size. Set your miter saw to 45 degrees and cut the crown molding upside down, leaning against the fence (Photo 6). Also miter a "tester" section of molding to help you position the sidepieces when you nail them in place. To avoid splitting, be sure to predrill nail holes. With the sides in place, add the front piece of crown molding. Cut it slightly long and then "shave" one end with your miter saw until it fits perfectly. Add the molding to the base frame the same way. Screw both the crown and base to the cabinet (Photo 8).

A quick finish

Brushing paint onto louvered doors is slow, fussy work, but you can avoid that hassle by using aerosol-can primer and paint. First, remove the doors and hinges. Cover the dowels, nails and screw heads with wood filler and sand the filler smooth. Also fill any voids in the plywood's edges. Sand the cabinet box, crown, base and doors with 120-grit paper. Spray all the parts with a white stain-blocking primer (such as BIN, Cover Stain or KILZ). When the primer dries, sand it lightly with a fine sanding sponge. Finally, spray on at least two coats of spray paint. High-gloss paint will accentuate every tiny surface flaw, so consider using satin or matte.

To hang the cabinet, locate studs and drive two 3-in. screws through the top cleat. Then rehang the doors. Close the doors to check their fit. Nudge the bottom of the cabinet left or right to square it and align the doors. Then drive screws through the bottom cleat.

Store-bought closet doors keep it fast and simple

Building cabinet doors is a tricky, time-consuming job. But you can avoid all that fussy work by buying closet doors and cutting them to fit the cabinet. Here you'll learn a fast, foolproof way to hang the doors using special hinges.

7 **Magazine storage** bins

Build these bins and stock them with an orderly archive, and you'll have instant access to years of your favorite magazines. You can build four bins from one 2 x 4-ft. sheet of 1/4-in. plywood and two 6-ft.-long 1x4s. Here's how:

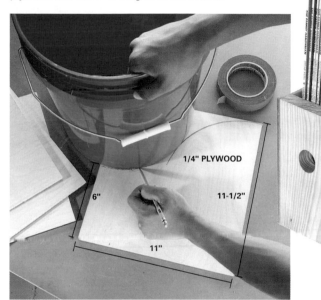

1/4" PLYWOOD

6"   11-1/2"

11"

1 Cut the 1/4-in. plywood into eight 11-1/2-in. x 11-in. pieces. Use a 5-gallon bucket to trace a graceful S-curve from the 11-1/2-in.-high corner across the plywood to a 6-in. mark on the opposite side. Simply establish a smooth curve.

TWO TAPED TOGETHER

2 Stack pairs so the best sides face each other and tape all the sheets together flush at the edges. "Gang cut" the curve with a jigsaw or a band saw.

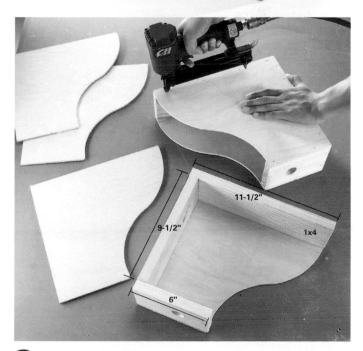

11-1/2"

9-1/2"   1x4

6"

3 Saw pine boards into 6-, 9-1/2- and 11-1/2-in. lengths. Drill 1-in.-diameter finger pulls in the 6-in. pieces, then nail the frames together. Nail the sides to the frames with 1-in. finish nails, sand as needed and apply a finish.

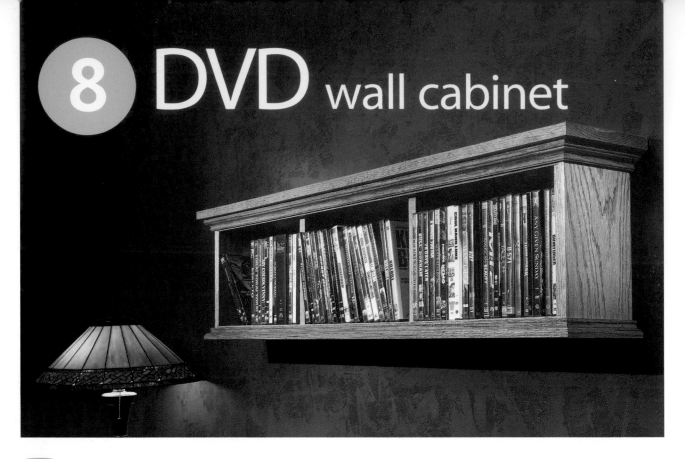

⑧ DVD wall cabinet

Do you have DVDs scattered all over the room? This handsome cabinet is one solution to the clutter. As shown, the cabinet is 42 in. wide and holds about 60 DVD cases. Go ahead and expand or shrink the width to better hold your collection or to fit a particular spot on the wall. The construction techniques will be the same no matter the width. Shown here are simple cutting and joining techniques that'll deliver fine cabinet-quality results. Read on to learn how to make clean and accurate crosscuts, rabbets (grooves on edges), and miters so you'll wind up with a spectacular finished product.

You don't need any special woodworking skills to complete this project, but you will need a table saw. To get good, true, splinter-free results, buy a 40-tooth carbide blade. If you have a pneumatic nailer, use it with 1-1/2-in. brads to fasten the cabinet parts and 1-in. brads to nail the cornice. This will speed up the assembly and give better results than hand nailing. Expect to spend about $65 for all the hardwood you'll need.

Choose the wood to match your decor

This cabinet is made of oak and finished with oil stain (Minwax "Golden Oak") and shellac. Make your cabinet from whatever wood best matches your room's decor. But if you choose wood other than poplar, oak or pine, be aware that the home center probably won't stock matching molding for the top and bottom. If you choose paint for the finish, select poplar boards and clear pine molding.

Rip the parts to width first, then to length

Begin by ripping the two 6-ft.-long 1x8s to 6 in. wide, then crosscut the end and top and bottom boards to length as shown

(Figure B). Go ahead and rip the divider panels to the final 5-in. width, but hold off on cutting the dividers and top cap to length for now. Cut those when you assemble the cabinet frame so you can measure and cut for perfect fits (Photo 9).

The key to clean tight joints is to make matching pairs of parts exactly the same length. A table saw works best, but you could use a miter box instead.

The small fence that comes with your miter gauge isn't much good for holding wood square to make accurate cuts. Extend it by screwing a 24-in.-long fence extension to the miter gauge, with the right side hanging a bit past the blade (Photo 1). (There are holes in the miter gauge just for this task.) One of the leftover pieces from your previous rips will work great for the extension fence. Choose screw lengths that penetrate the wood about 5/8 in. after allowing for the miter gauge wall thickness.

Don't trust the angle indicators on your miter gauge; they're bound to be inaccurate. Instead, square the miter gauge to one of the miter gauge slots with a carpenter's square (Photo 1). When it's square, tighten up the locking handle. Raise the blade and cut off the end of the fence and you're ready to crosscut. The end of the fence perfectly marks the saw blade's path. Line up measurement marks with that end and you'll know exactly where to place the board for cutting.

Nest the wood against the miter gauge clear of the blade, start up the saw, and push the wood all the way past the blade. To be safe, shut off the saw before removing both parts.

Cut the rabbets

Now cut the 3/8-in.-deep, 1/4-in.-wide rabbets on the back of the bottom, top and sides to create a recess for the 1/4-in.-thick plywood back (Photo 3). First lower the blade below the throat plate and clamp a straight 3/4-in.-thick sacrificial board to the saw fence.

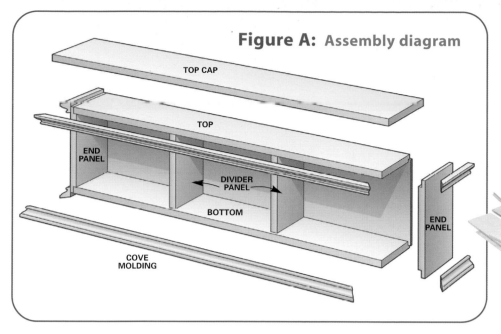

Figure A: Assembly diagram

TOP CAP

TOP

END PANEL

DIVIDER PANEL

BOTTOM

END PANEL

COVE MOLDING

Build this project from three boards, a little plywood and 12 ft. of trim.

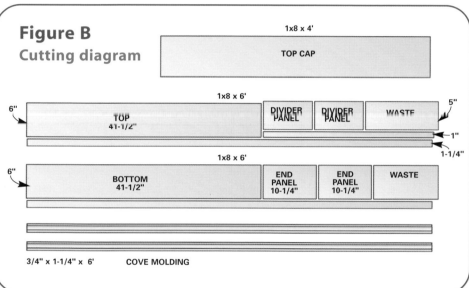

Figure B
Cutting diagram

1x8 x 4'
TOP CAP

1x8 x 6'
6"
TOP
4'1-1/2"
DIVIDER PANEL
DIVIDER PANEL
WASTE
5"
1"
1-1/4"

1x8 x 6'
6"
BOTTOM
41-1/2"
END PANEL 10-1/4"
END PANEL 10-1/4"
WASTE

3/4" x 1-1/4" x 6'   COVE MOLDING

Materials list

- Two 6' 1x8s: Cabinet top and bottom, end panels and center dividers.
- One 4' 1x8: Top cap
- Two 6' lengths of 3/4" x 1-1/4" cove molding: Top and bottom trim
- 2 x 4' 1/4" plywood: Back panel (not shown)

Position the clamps at least 1 in. above the table so the 3/4-in. boards can slide under them. Move the fence over the blade so it will cut about 1/8 in. into the sacrificial board, then lock the fence, turn on the saw and slowly raise the blade into the board until it's about 1 in. above the table to cut a clearance slot (Photo 3). Lower the blade to 3/8 in. above the table to start cutting the rabbets.

Nudge the fence about 1/16 in. away from the blade and make cuts on all four boards (Photo 3). Be sure to hold the boards tight to the fence and the table for smooth, complete cuts. And keep your hands well away from the blade, because you have to remove the guard to make this cut. Continue moving the fence in 1/16-in. increments and making cuts until you approach the final 1/4-in. depth of the rabbet. Then check the depth with 1/4-in. plywood and make fine adjustments in the fence to make a final cut. The plywood should fit flush with the back edge of the board.

Leave the depth setting on the blade and use the miter gauge to cut the rabbets on the end panels. Set the fence to cut 3/4 in. wide (measured to the far edge of the blade). Make a series of cuts at each end (Photo 4). Push the wood completely through

and stop the saw before pulling the miter gauge back. The more passes and the narrower you make them, the less you'll need to clean up the saw kerfs later. Smooth any saw marks with a sharp chisel for a cleaner-looking, tighter-fitting joint (Photo 5).

Sand all the surfaces up to 120 grit for open-grain woods like oak, pine, cherry and walnut. And sand to 220 grit for closed-grain woods like maple and birch.

Stain before assembly

If you're staining, stain the parts at this point because it's tough to get into inside corners after you assemble the cabinet. For stronger glue joints, cover the surfaces of the rabbets with masking tape to keep stain off (Photo 6). Cut the plywood back about 1/2 in. larger than the opening, prefinish it at the same time and cut it to exact size later along with the center dividers.

This step will give you better finishing results, but it will add to the project completion time because it means letting stains dry before assembly. If you're determined to complete the cabinet in one shop visit, go ahead and assemble it, then stain and finish it afterward.

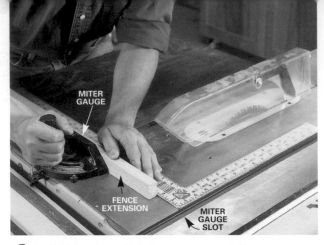

1 Screw a 2-ft.-long extension fence to the miter gauge. Square the miter gauge with the miter gauge slot.

2 Rip the boards to width (use Figure B for cutting dimensions), then cut the top, bottom and sides to length.

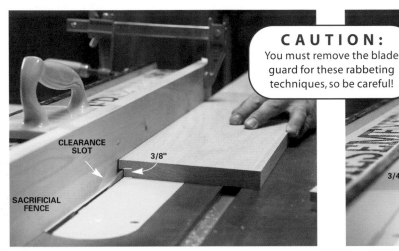

C A U T I O N :
You must remove the blade guard for these rabbeting techniques, so be careful!

3 Set the blade to cut 3/8 in. deep. Make a series of passes along the back edge of each board, moving the fence away from the blade with each pass until the width is 1/4 in.

4 Set the fence 3/4 in. from the far edge of the blade and make a series of 3/8-in.-deep overlapping saw kerfs to rabbet the top and bottom of the end panels.

Assemble the sides, dividers and back

Glue and nail each end panel to the top and bottom boards. Four 1-in. brads, two at the top and two at the bottom, are plenty. Then clamp the assembly together to pull the joints tight (Photo 7). Check for square right away before the glue sets. You'll need clamps that are at least 5 ft. long for this. Use blocks to spread the pressure over the whole joint. If one of the diagonal measurements is longer than the other, gently squeeze another clamp across those corners to pull the frame square. If you don't have long clamps, just glue and clamp the joints together with a few extra brads. (The joints might not be as tightly fit as clamped ones, but you can plug slim gaps with wood filler later.) Measure and cut the back to fit, then glue and nail it in place with 1-in. brads spaced every 6 in. (Photo 8).

Save the dividers for last. Measure and cut them to fit, then space them equally in the cabinet and nail them through the top and bottom with 1-1/2-in. brads (Photo 9). No glue is needed.

Add the cove trim and top cap

Cut and install the cove molding starting at one end, then the long front piece, then the other end. To get perfect final lengths (Photo 11), cut 45-degree bevels on a short piece of molding to use as a test block when you're fitting and cutting. Use your miter gauge to cut the bevels. The technique is the same as crosscutting, only with the saw blade set to 45 degrees (Photo 10). Leave 3/16 in. of "reveal" (exposed cabinet edge) for a nice look. You can go with a wider or narrower reveal as long as it's consistent. Fasten the molding to the cabinet with glue and 1-in. brads.

Center the top cap on either side of the molding and flush with the back, then glue and pin it to the molding with 1-1/2-in. brads (Photo 12). Place the brads carefully over the thick part of the trim. It's easy to accidentally blow through the narrower, contoured front.

Clear-coat the cabinet with the finish of your choice. It's easier to apply smooth coats of finish with a spray can than with a brush, especially when you're finishing the interior. Shown here are three coats of shellac. It dries quickly, so you can completely finish (all three coats) in one day. It's also the least hazardous of all finishes. Do your spraying in a dust-free room and you won't even have to sand between coats.

Hang it on the wall

With a 42-in. cabinet, you should be able to hang it with 2-1/2-in. screws driven through the back and into two studs. But if you can only find one stud, use drywall anchors near the end farthest from the stud.

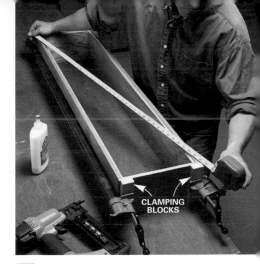

5 Smooth the saw marks by shaving the rabbets flat with a sharp chisel.

6 Cover the rabbets with masking tape and apply stain to all the cabinet parts.

7 Glue and nail the end panels to the top and bottom. Then clamp the assembly and check for square.

8 Cut the back panel to fit, then glue and nail it into the rabbets with 1-in. brads.

9 Measure and cut the center dividers to fit. Then space them equally and nail them with 1-1/2-in. brads.

10 Cut the moldings to length using the miter gauge with the saw blade set at a 45-degree bevel.

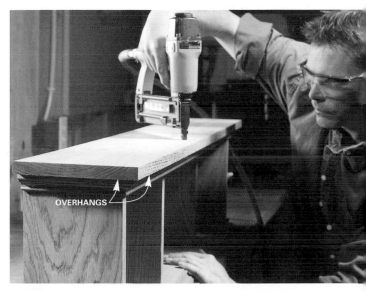

11 Use a scrap of cove molding to test-fit lengths. Glue and nail the molding with 1-in. brads.

12 Cut the top cap to length so that the end overhangs match the front. Then glue the top cap to the molding and nail with 1-1/2-in. brads.

9 Coat and mitten rack

This coat rack is easy to build with butt joints connected by screws that get hidden with wooden screw-hole buttons and wood plugs. It mounts easily to the wall with screws driven through the hidden hanging strip on the back. The five large Shaker pegs are great for holding hats, umbrellas and coats, and the hinged-hatch door at the top keeps the clutter of gloves and scarfs from view.

Maple is an ideal wood for Shaker-style pieces, but any hardwood will do. Figure on spending about $60 for wood, hardware and varnish.

Cutting the pieces

First transfer the pattern measurements in Figure A, p. 25 (using a compass) and then cut the sides (A) with a jigsaw. Next cut the top (D) to length and rip the shelf (B) to the width given in the Cutting list, p. 25. Cut the hanging strip (F) and the peg strip (C) to the same length as the shelf (B). Now drill the 3/8-in. counterbore holes for the screw-hole buttons (with your spade bit) 3/16 in. deep into the outsides of parts A (as shown in Figure A, and Photo 2). Also drill the 3/8-in. counterbore holes in the top. These holes *must* be 3/8 in. deep.

Mark and drill the 1/2-in. holes for the Shaker pegs in the peg strip. Drill the holes for the Shaker pegs perfectly perpendicular to the peg strip to ensure they all project evenly when glued in place.

Assembly

Lay the pieces on your workbench, as shown in Photo 3. Align the hanging strip (F), the shelf (B), and the peg strip (C) as shown and clamp the sides (A) to these parts. Predrill the holes with a combination pilot hole/countersink bit using the center of the counterbore holes as a guide. Next, screw the sides to B, C and F. Fasten the top (D) to the sides in the same manner.

Glue and clamp the hatch stops to the insides of parts A, as shown in Figure A. To finish the assembly, cut the hatch (E) to size and install the hinges to the underside of part D and the top of the hatch. Now glue the buttons and pegs into their corresponding holes. Use only a small drop of glue for the buttons but be

NOTE: Be sure this project is screwed to the wall studs. Drill two holes into the hanging strip at stud locations and use 2-1/2-in. or longer wood screws.

sure to apply a thin layer of glue completely around the plugs. This will swell the plugs for a tight fit.

Finishing

Lightly sand the entire piece after assembly with 220-grit sandpaper. Apply two coats of clear Danish oil to all the surfaces (remove the hinges and knobs). Once the finish is dry, add two magnetic catches to the hatch-stop molding (G).

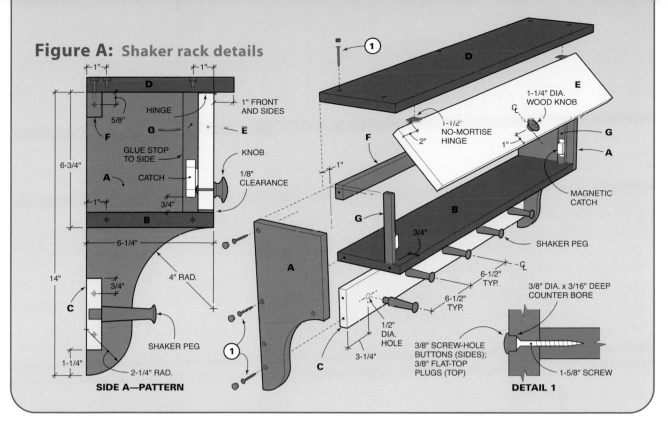

Figure A: Shaker rack details

SIDE A—PATTERN

- 1"
- D
- 1"
- HINGE
- 5/8"
- F
- G
- GLUE STOP TO SIDE
- A
- CATCH
- 6-3/4"
- 1" FRONT AND SIDES
- E
- KNOB
- 1/8" CLEARANCE
- 1"
- B
- 3/4"
- 6-1/4"
- 14"
- 4" RAD.
- C
- 3/4"
- SHAKER PEG
- 1-1/4"
- 2-1/4" RAD.

- 1
- D
- E
- 1-1/4" DIA. WOOD KNOB
- G
- 1-1/2" NO-MORTISE HINGE
- 2"
- F
- G
- 1"
- A
- G
- MAGNETIC CATCH
- 1"
- 3/4"
- B
- SHAKER PEG
- A
- 6-1/2" TYP.
- 6-1/2" TYP.
- 3/8" DIA. x 3/16" DEEP COUNTER BORE
- 1/2" DIA. HOLE
- 1
- 3-1/4"
- C
- 3/8" SCREW-HOLE BUTTONS (SIDES); 3/8" FLAT-TOP PLUGS (TOP)
- 1-5/8" SCREW
- DETAIL 1

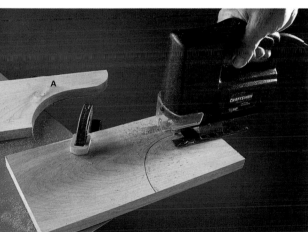

1 Cut the side pieces (A) using a jigsaw or hand saw. Sand the curved edges smooth.

Materials list

Item	Qty.
1-1/2" no-mortise hinges	1 pair
1-1/4" beech knob	1
narrow magnetic catch	2
3-3/8" long Shaker pegs	5
3/8" screw-hole buttons	10
3/8" plugs	5
3/8" spade bit	1
1/2" spade bit	1
1-5/8" wood screws	15
Wood glue	1 pint
Danish oil	1 pint
150- and 220-grit sandpaper	

2 Drill the 1/2-in. holes 5/8 in. deep for the 3-3/8-in. Shaker pegs and the 3/8-in. counterbore holes 3/16 in. deep for the screw-hole buttons in parts A.

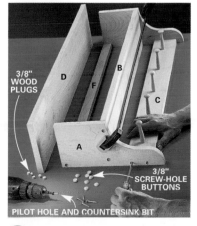

3 Assemble the shelf by clamping parts C, F and B to the sides. Drill pilot holes and screw the pieces together. The screws will be covered by the buttons and plugs.

Cutting list

Key	Pcs.	Size & description
A	2	3/4" x 6-1/4" x 14" maple sides
B	1	3/4" x 6-1/4" x 32-1/2" maple shelf
C	1	3/4" x 3-1/2" x 32-1/2" maple peg strip
D	1	3/4" x 7-1/4" x 36" maple top
E	1	3/4" x 5-13/16" x 32-5/16" maple hatch
F	1	3/4" x 1-1/4" x 32-1/2" maple hanging strip
G	2	3/4" x 1/2" x 6" maple hatch stop

10 Summer lounge chair

Most wooden outdoor chairs can get uncomfortable in a half hour. This one is designed so you can settle in and knock off a few magazines or even catch a snooze. The cushion adds an extra bit of staying power, and the slats will help keep you cool. And you'll like the built-in tray on the back for holding your snack and phone.

Every detail of this chair is engineered for simplicity of construction, starting with the use of standard-width lumber for the parts.

While a power miter box is ideal for cutting the parts to length, you could easily use a circular saw or even a jigsaw for all the cuts. You'll also need a drill/driver and spring clamps for assembly.

These chairs are pine, but you could choose fir, cedar, treated pine or any other wood that can handle the outdoors. The pine for each chair cost about $35. Order the cushion online (see Buyer's Guide, p. 28), or use any chair cushion about 18 to 20 in. square

Select the best boards

You'll need only 1x3s (3/4 in. x 2-1/2 in.) and 1x4s (3/4 in. x 3-1/2 in.) for this project. Choose wood that either is knot free or has only small tight knots. Look for straight boards, but they don't have to be perfect because you'll cut them into shorter lengths. If you can't find good 1x3s, buy 1x6s and rip 2-1/2-in.-wide pieces from them. You can ask the lumberyard to do it if you don't have access to a table saw.

Assemble the chair seat and back

Do all your assembly work on a flat benchtop or floor area in your garage or shop. Begin the process by cutting the seat box parts. It's easier to give the parts a quick sanding at this point than to sand the project after assembly. Then drill pilot and countersink holes and assemble the box with 1-5/8-in. deck screws. (See Photo 1 and Figure A.) A No. 8 pilot/countersink bit ($10) lets you quickly predrill and countersink in one step. Next cut the seat supports (C) using a miter saw or an angle guide to cut the 75-degree angle. An adjustable Quick Square (Stanley No. 46-050; $12 at hardware stores) works great as a cutting guide (Photo 2). Spread an exterior glue and screw the supports to the sides of the box with 1-1/4-in. galvanized screws (Photo 3).

Cut the seat back sides (E) and the seat top (B) and then glue and screw these pieces together with 1-5/8-in. deck screws. Next, glue and screw the back supports (D) to the seat back sides, making sure the supports extend 3-1/2 in. beyond the ends of the sides.

With the seat box assembly lying flat, insert the back assembly and align the back supports (D) directly behind the seat supports (C) and secure them with clamps (Photo 4). Drill two 1/4-in. holes through

each seat box side and through the back supports. Insert 1/4-in. x 2-in. carriage bolts, add a washer and tighten the nuts with a wrench.

Bolt the legs to the chair

Mark the legs and seat frame with an adjustable square set at 10 degrees. Then draw a 10-degree line on the sides of the seat

1 Cut the sides (A) and ends (B) for the seat box. Drill pilot and countersink holes and screw the box together with 1-5/8-in. deck screws.

Figure A: Lounge chair details

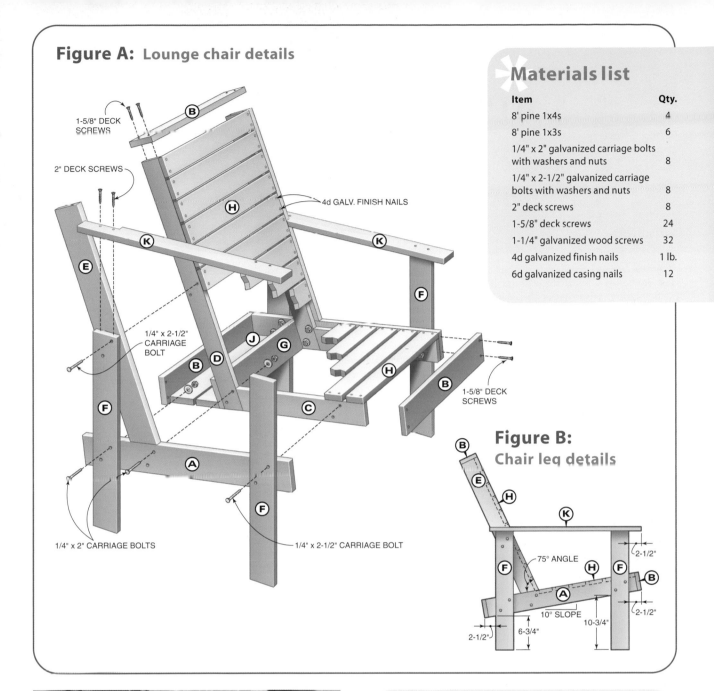

1-5/8" DECK SCREWS

2" DECK SCREWS

4d GALV. FINISH NAILS

1/4" x 2-1/2" CARRIAGE BOLT

1/4" x 2" CARRIAGE BOLTS

1/4" x 2-1/2" CARRIAGE BOLT

1-5/8" DECK SCREWS

Materials list

Item	Qty.
8' pine 1x4s	4
8' pine 1x3s	6
1/4" x 2" galvanized carriage bolts with washers and nuts	8
1/4" x 2-1/2" galvanized carriage bolts with washers and nuts	8
2" deck screws	8
1-5/8" deck screws	24
1-1/4" galvanized wood screws	32
4d galvanized finish nails	1 lb.
6d galvanized casing nails	12

Figure B: Chair leg details

75° ANGLE

10° SLOPE

2-1/2"

2-1/2"

6-3/4"

10-3/4"

2-1/2"

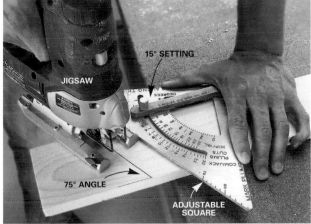

JIGSAW

15° SETTING

75° ANGLE

ADJUSTABLE SQUARE

2 Cut accurate angles for the seat supports (C), using an adjustable angle guide as a straightedge to guide your jigsaw or circular saw.

Cutting list

Key	Qty.	Size & description
A	2	3/4" x 3-1/2" x 30" seat box sides
B	3	3/4" x 3-1/2" x 21-1/2" seat top and box ends
C	2	3/4" x 2-1/2" x 19-1/2" seat supports (measure to long point of 75° angle)
D	2	3/4" x 2-1/2" x 32-9/16" back supports (measure to long point of 75° angle)
E	2	3/4" x 3-1/2" x 29-1/8" seat back sides (measure to long point of 75° angle)
F	4	3/4" x 3-1/2" x 23-1/2" legs
G	1	3/4" x 3-1/2" x 20" back seat brace
H	17	3/4" x 2-1/2" x 20" seat and back slats
J	2	3/4" x 3-1/2" x 20" storage tray slats
K	2	3/4" x 2-1/2" x 30" arms

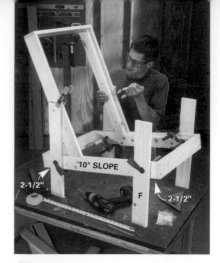

3 Glue and screw the seat supports (C) to the sides of the seat box (A) with 1-1/4-in. galvanized screws. Wipe off excess glue that squeezes out.

4 Cut, drill and assemble the parts for the back (Figure A). Then clamp the back to the seat frame, drill 1/4-in. holes and install the carriage bolts.

5 Position the legs and clamp them to the frame using Figure B as a guide. Drill and fasten them with carriage bolts. Nail the rear storage tray slats to the sides.

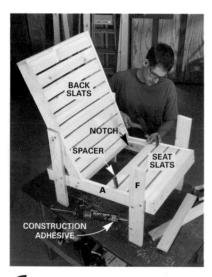

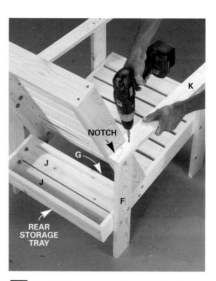

6 Cut the seat and back slats to length. Glue and nail them with 4d galvanized finish nails. Use two spacers to ensure consistent gaps.

7 Notch the arms to fit around the seat back frame. Then predrill and fasten the arms to the front and rear legs with 2-in. deck screws.

8 Soak the legs overnight in a wood preservative or an oil-based deck stain to slow water absorption. Once the legs are dry, prime and paint.

frame, 2-1/2 in. from the front and back (Figure B), to mark the leg positions. Also mark on the back edge of the rear legs at 6-3/4 in. and on the back edge of the front legs at 10-3/4 in. (Figure B).

Align the marks on the legs and the seat frame and clamp the parts into place (Photo 5). Be sure the front and back legs are parallel and that both legs are square to the work surface. Clamp the legs to the seat frame and the back. Drill 1/4-in. holes and bolt the legs to the seat and back. Cut the two slats (J) for the rear shelf and the back seat brace (G) and nail them to the sides with 6d galvanized casing nails.

Nail the seat and back slats

Cut the slats (H) for the seat and back. Starting at the top of the seat back, fasten the slats with glue and 4d (1-1/2-in.) galvanized finish nails. The 1x3s used here were 2-5/8 in. wide and spaced every 3/8 in. If your 1x3s are narrower, adjust the spacing or add another slat. You'll probably have to notch the lowest slat on the back to fit around the seat supports (Photo 6).

Now glue and nail the seat slats to the seat supports, starting at the front. Adjust the spacing to get a good fit.

To complete the chair, cut the arms and hold each on top of the legs so it overhangs the corresponding front leg 2-1/2 in. Then mark the back of the arm and notch it 3/4 in. with your jigsaw so it fits tightly against the side of the seat back (Photo 7). Fasten the arms so the outer sides overhang the legs by 1 in.

No matter what finish you choose, be sure to soak the legs in a preservative or deck stain to keep water from wicking up and ruining the finish or causing rot (Photo 8). If you paint, use an oil-based primer followed by two topcoats of a high-quality gloss or semigloss acrylic paint.

Buyer's Guide

You can find chair cushions at Home Decorators (877-537-8539; www.homedecorators.com). Choose from simple seat cushion No. 26106 or full seat and back No. 26107 in a wide variety of patterns and colors. Two other sources are Domestications (800-826-8240; www.domestications.com) and Cushion Source (800-510-8325; www.cushionsource.com). Cushion Source will make custom cushions in any size.

Saw blade carryall

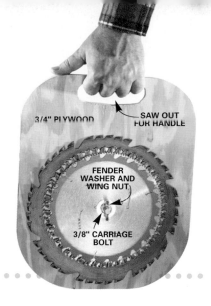

3/4" PLYWOOD

SAW OUT FOR HANDLE

FENDER WASHER AND WING NUT

3/8" CARRIAGE BOLT

This carryall is perfect for storing and toting table and circular saw blades. Cut a 14-in. x 12-in. piece of 3/4-in. plywood and drill a hole for a 2-in. x 3/8-in. carriage bolt. Secure the blades on the bolt with a fender washer and wing nut, being careful to stagger the carbide teeth so they don't rub together. Saw a slot in the upper end for a handle and for storing it on pegboard.

Air compressor cart

Build this mobile home for your small air compressor and roll it to any job, any where in the shop, house or yard! The built-in air hose reel and tool bin keep your whole air-powered tool operation together. Measure your compressor before building. You may have to alter the dimensions so yours will fit.

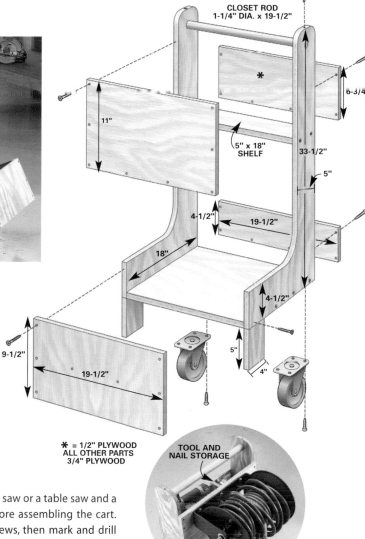

CLOSET ROD 1-1/4" DIA. x 19-1/2"

6-3/4"

11"

5" x 18" SHELF

*

33-1/2"

5"

4-1/2"

19-1/2"

18"

4-1/2"

9-1/2"

5"

4"

19-1/2"

* = 1/2" PLYWOOD ALL OTHER PARTS 3/4" PLYWOOD

TOOL AND NAIL STORAGE

You'll need:

- Two 2-ft. x 4-ft. sheets of 3/4-in. plywood ($8 each at a home center)
- One 2-ft. x 4-ft. sheet of 1/2-in. plywood
- One 1-1/4-in. closet dowel
- Two 4-in. casters ($8 each at a home center)
- One air hose reel ($37; part no. 159184 at www.northerntool.com)
- Six 3/8-in. x 2-in. hex head bolts, nuts and washers
- Eight 5/16-in. x 1-in. lag screws

Cut out the plywood parts (see illustration) with a circular saw or a table saw and a jigsaw for the curves. Bore the 1-1/4-in. dowel holes before assembling the cart. Mount casters to the underside of the base with lag screws, then mark and drill holes in the crosspiece for the hose reel and bolt it on. That's it! Organize nail guns, nail packs, nail gun oil and tire inflation accessories in the handy tool pockets and you're ready to roll.

13 Behind-the-door shelves

The space behind a door is another storage spot that's often overlooked. Build a set of shallow shelves and mount it to the wall. The materials cost about $40. Measure the distance between the door hinge and the wall and subtract 1 in. This is the maximum depth of the shelves. This project uses 1x4s for the sides, top and shelves. Screw the sides to the top. Then screw three 1x2 hanging strips to the sides: one top and bottom and one centered. Nail metal shelf standards to the sides. Complete the shelves by nailing a 1x2 trim piece to the sides and top. The 1x2 dresses up the shelf unit and keeps the shelves from falling off the shelf clips.

Locate the studs. Drill clearance holes and screw the shelves to the studs with 2-1/2-in. wood screws. Put a rubber bumper on the frame to protect the door.

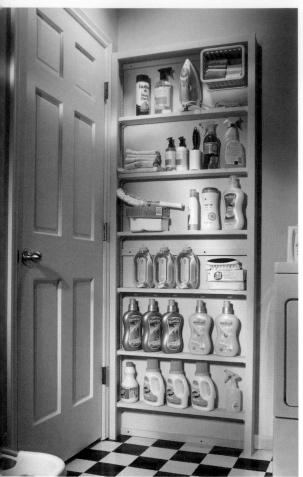

Build shallow shelves to fit behind the door in your laundry room, utility room or pantry.

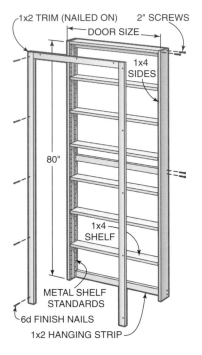

1x2 TRIM (NAILED ON) 2" SCREWS
DOOR SIZE
1x4 SIDES
80"
1x4 SHELF
METAL SHELF STANDARDS
6d FINISH NAILS
1x2 HANGING STRIP

14 Glass shower shelf

Tired of the clutter of shampoo and conditioner bottles along the rim of your tub? This tempered safety glass shelf on a cable shelf bracket is an easy solution. The cable shelf bracket requires only two screws for support. If studs aren't located in the right positions, use toggle bolts to anchor the shelf brackets. The glass hangs on the cables. The cable shelf brackets (No. CSB5B) are available online from www.expodesigninc.com and cost $21 per pair. Order a tempered glass shelf from a local glass company. The 3/8-in.-thick, 12-in.-deep shelf shown here cost $64.

Mount a shelf above your tub to store towels, shampoo and conditioner.

15 Shoe-storage **booster stool**

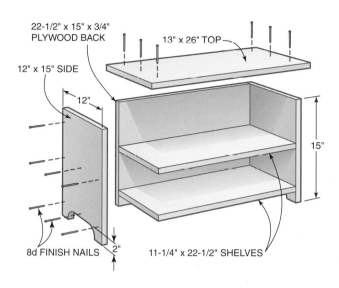

Build this double-duty step stool from six pieces of 3/4-in. plywood.

22-1/2" x 15" x 3/4" PLYWOOD BACK

13" x 26" TOP

12" x 15" SIDE

12"

15"

8d FINISH NAILS

2"

11-1/4" x 22-1/2" SHELVES

Build this handy stool in one hour and park it in your closet. You can also use it as a step to reach the high shelf. All you need is a 4x4 sheet of 3/4-in. plywood, wood glue and a handful of 8d finish nails. Cut the plywood pieces according to the illustration. Spread wood glue on the joints, then nail them together with 8d finish nails. First nail through the sides into the back. Then nail through the top into the sides and back. Finally, mark the location of the two shelves and nail through the sides into the shelves.

16 **Tool** tote

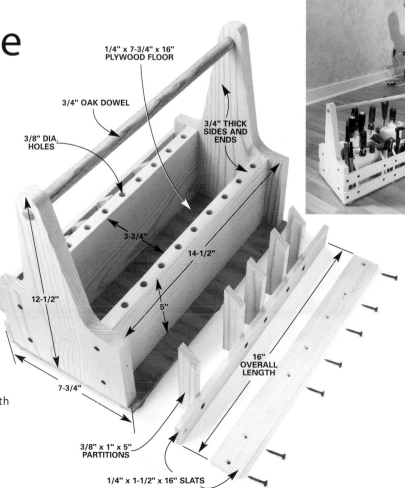

1/4" x 7-3/4" x 16" PLYWOOD FLOOR

3/4" OAK DOWEL

3/8" DIA. HOLES

3/4" THICK SIDES AND ENDS

3-3/4"

14-1/2"

12-1/2"

5"

7-3/4"

16" OVERALL LENGTH

3/8" x 1" x 5" PARTITIONS

1/4" x 1-1/2" x 16" SLATS

Keep all your hand tools within easy reach in a portable 16-in. pine carton. Build one from a 1x8 x 12-ft. pine board, 1/4-in. plywood and a 3/4-in. oak dowel, and you'll never run back to the garage for a bit, blade, wrench or nail. Here's how:

■ Cut and screw together the sides and ends with the ends protruding 1 in. beyond the sides. Drill holes in the top of the ends for a 3/4-in. dowel handle and tap it in the holes before assembling the ends and sides. Drill the 3/8-in. storage holes in the top edges of the sides before assembly.

■ Saw 1/4-in. x 1-1/2-in. pine strips for the side slats and screw them to the protruding ends.

■ Cut and screw on the 1/4-in. plywood floor.

■ Cut 3/8-in. pine partitions and screw them behind the side slats to create custom-width pockets for the tools.

17 Chopping board and serving tray

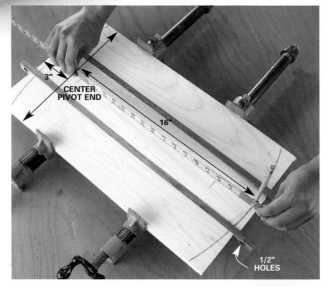

Slice, dice and serve in style on this easy, cutting-edge project. Here you'll learn a simple way to dry-fit the parts, scribe the arc and then glue the whole thing together. A 4-ft. steel ruler is used to scribe the arcs, but a yardstick or any thin board would also work. Be sure to use water-resistant wood glue and keep your tray out of the dishwasher or it might fall apart. And one more thing: Keep the boards as even as possible during glue-up to minimize sanding later.

Materials list

- Three 20-in. x 3-1/2-in. maple boards
- Two 23-1/2-in. x 1/2-in. x 3/4-in. walnut strips (handle strips)
- Two 5-in. x 1/2-in.-diameter dowels (handles)
- Four 3/4-in. x 3/4-in.-diameter dowels (for feet)

1 Drill 1/2-in. holes centered 3/4 in. in from the ends of the walnut strips. Then lightly clamp all five boards together so you can scribe the arcs on the ends.

2 Take the boards out of the clamp, saw and sand the arcs on each board, and then glue the assembly together, leaving the dowel handles unglued.

3 Unclamp, sand both sides and drill a 1/4-in.-deep, 3/4-in.-diameter hole at each underside corner. Glue in the feet and dowel handles, then wipe on a couple of coats of Butcher Block Oil ($7.00 at www.rockler.com).

18 Stacked recycling tower

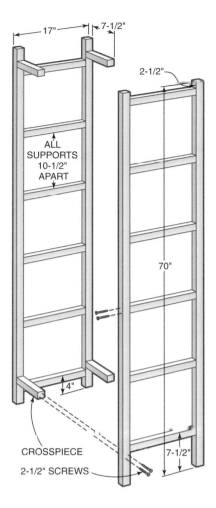

F ive plastic containers, six 2x2s and screws, and one hour's work are all it takes to put together this space-saving recycling storage rack. The frame fits containers that have a top that measures 14-1/2 in. x 10 in. and are 15 in. tall. The containers shown here were made by Rubbermaid.

If you use different-size containers, adjust the distance between the uprights so the 2x2s will catch the lip of the container. Then adjust the spacing of the horizontal rungs for a snug fit when the container is angled as shown.

Start by cutting the 2x2s to length according to the illustration. Then mark the position of the rungs on the uprights. Drill two 5/32-in. holes through the uprights at each crosspiece position. Drill from the outside to the inside and angle the holes inward slightly to prevent the screws from breaking out the side of the rungs.

Drive 2-1/2-in. screws through the uprights into the rungs. Assemble the front and back frames. Then connect them with the side crosspieces.

Build a space-saving tower for plastic recycling containers with simple 2x2 and screw construction.

19 Sandwich-bag parts organizer

Cut slots in a piece of plywood with a jigsaw. Fill resealable bags with small parts, hardware or craft items and hang them from the slotted plywood.

K eep screws, connectors, nails and other small parts in sight and handy with this resealable bag holder. You can build it out of a 3/4-in.-thick scrap of plywood. Start by cutting two pieces of plywood as shown. Draw lines 1 in. apart across the shorter piece with a square, stopping 1 in. from the edge. Now cut along the lines with a jigsaw. Screw the two pieces of plywood together and screw the unit to the wall. Fill resealable bags and slip them into the slots.

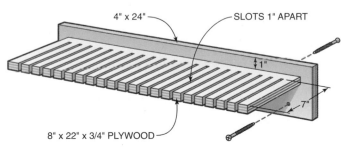

20 Catch-all cabinet

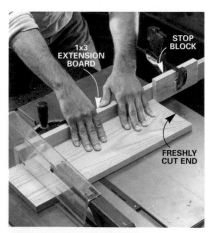

Craft supplies, CDs, kids' books, household tools—everyone's got a collection of something that needs to be stored. And this cabinet is perfect for the job. It's designed with simple joints and details so you can assemble it in a morning, even if you don't have any cabinet-building experience. All of the cutting can be done on a table saw.

Buy everything at the home center

Buy two 8-ft. long 1x8s, one 2x4 sheet of 1/4-in. plywood, a pair of offset hinges, four 36-in. x 5/8-in. shelf standards and a door pull. This cabinet is made of red oak that's been stained with Watco golden oak finishing oil and topcoated with satin polyurethane (two coats). If you want to paint it, buy basswood or aspen along with birch plywood for the panel and back. That way the grain won't show through the paint.

Use a table saw and accessories

You can build this cabinet with any table saw ranging from a $150 8-in. portable to a 10-in. cabinet saw that costs $1,800. If you have an inexpensive saw, spend more time making sure fences and miter gauges are square and aligned during each setup.

To take full advantage of any table saw, invest in a good blade, a set of dado blades and a few special accessories to ensure safe, accurate work:

- Get a 40-tooth carbide combination blade (about $50) for end cutting and for ripping widths.
- Make or buy a featherboard to hold wood snugly against the fence for smoother, safer cuts (Photo 9).
- A push pad (Photo 5) and push stick (Photo 9) keep your hands clear of the blade and the wood flat against the saw table.

- A set of 6-in. dado blades ($60 and up) works great for cutting grooves (rabbets and dadoes). You'll need a special throat plate with a wider blade opening to accommodate the dado blade. Buy one that fits your saw brand and model.

Cut the width, length and joints

Get started by ripping all the boards to width and then rough-cutting the sides and tops of the cabinet box to length (1 in. or so too long) using Figure B as a guide. Turn the ripped edges of the side and top boards toward the back of the cabinet to hide the saw marks.

Cut the dadoes and rabbets with the dado blade. A rabbet is simply a groove on the edge of a board. Set up the dado blade to cut

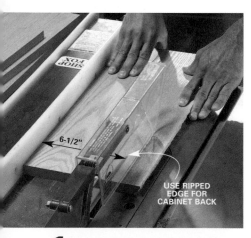

1 Cut the box's side, top and bottom boards to rough length (1 in. or so too long), then rip them to width (see Figure B).

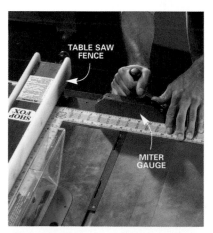

2 Square the miter gauge to the table saw fence with a carpenter's square and tighten the lockdown handle.

3 Screw a straight 1x3 extension board to the miter gauge and then cut cabinet sides, bottom and top boards to length. Use a stop block for repetitive cuts.

Figure A
Cabinet assembly

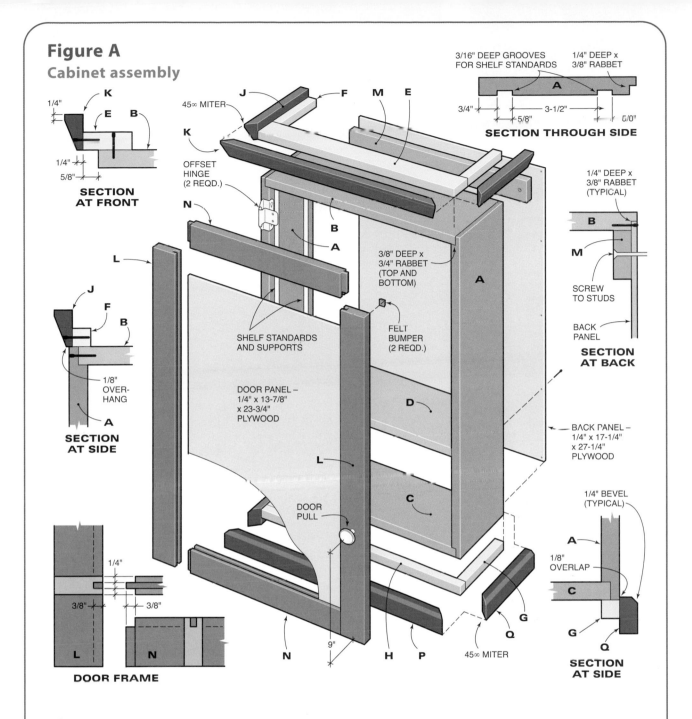

3/16" DEEP GROOVES FOR SHELF STANDARDS

1/4" DEEP x 3/8" RABBET

A

3/4"   3-1/2"   5/8"   5/8"

SECTION THROUGH SIDE

K

1/4"

E   **B**

1/4"

5/8"

SECTION AT FRONT

J   45° MITER   **F**   **M**   **E**

K

OFFSET HINGE (2 REQD.)

N

B

A

1/4" DEEP x 3/8" RABBET (TYPICAL)

B

M

SCREW TO STUDS

BACK PANEL

SECTION AT BACK

L

J

F

B

1/8" OVER-HANG

A

SECTION AT SIDE

3/8" DEEP x 3/4" RABBET (TOP AND BOTTOM)

FELT BUMPER (2 REQD.)

SHELF STANDARDS AND SUPPORTS

DOOR PANEL – 1/4" x 13-7/8" x 23-3/4" PLYWOOD

D

A

BACK PANEL – 1/4" x 17-1/4" x 27-1/4" PLYWOOD

L

C

DOOR PULL

1/4" BEVEL (TYPICAL)

A

1/8" OVERLAP

C

G

Q

SECTION AT SIDE

1/4"

3/8"   3/8"

L   **N**

DOOR FRAME

9"

N   **H**   **P**   45° MITER   **G**   **Q**

Figure B
Cutting diagram

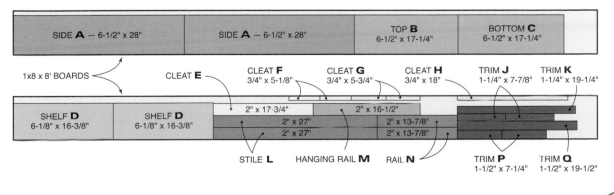

| SIDE **A** — 6-1/2" x 28" | SIDE **A** — 6-1/2" x 28" | TOP **B** 6-1/2" x 17-1/4" | BOTTOM **C** 6-1/2" x 17-1/4" |

1x8 x 8' BOARDS

CLEAT **E**

CLEAT **F** 3/4" x 5-1/8"

CLEAT **G** 3/4" x 5-3/4"

CLEAT **H** 3/4" x 18"

TRIM **J** 1-1/4" x 7-7/8"

TRIM **K** 1-1/4" x 19-1/4"

| SHELF **D** 6-1/8" x 16-3/8" | SHELF **D** 6-1/8" x 16-3/8" | 2" x 17-3/4" | 2" x 16-1/2" | |

2" x 27"   2" x 13-7/8"

2" x 27"   2" x 13-7/8"

STILE **L**   HANGING RAIL **M**   RAIL **N**   TRIM **P** 1-1/2" x 7-1/4"   TRIM **Q** 1-1/2" x 19-1/2"

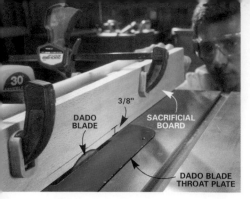

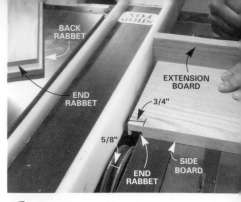

4 Mount a dado blade in the saw. Clamp a sacrificial board to the fence, start the saw and slowly raise the blade into the board until it's 3/8 in. above the saw table.

5 Readjust the fence to cut a 1/4-in.-wide rabbet and cut the rabbets for the back panel into the side, top and bottom. Push down firmly with a push pad to make a smooth cut.

6 Set the fence to cut 3/4 in. wide, then reset the miter gauge extension board to ride against the fence. Cut 3/4-in. rabbets on both ends of the box sides by making two overlapping passes.

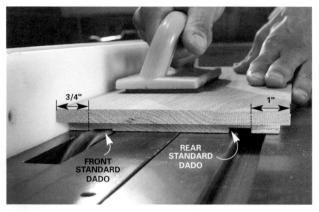

7 Lower the blade and cut 3/16-in.-deep dadoes to receive the shelf standards in the side boards, holding the boards down firmly with the push pad.

8 Apply glue to the rabbets, then clamp the box and nail the joints. Glue and nail on the hanging rail. Nail on the plywood back to square the box.

a 5/8-in.-wide groove. You can use the same setup for cutting the rabbet that receives the 1/4-in. plywood back (Photo 5), the rabbet in the top and bottom ends of the side boards (Photo 6) and the shelf standard dadoes. You'll only have to adjust the cutting depth, the table saw fence and miter gauge board for each cut as needed.

Fence and miter gauge extension boards

Clamp a 1x4 to the table saw fence to use as a "sacrificial" fence board when cutting rabbets in edges and ends (Photo 4). By raising the dado blade into the board to the proper depth (Photo 4), you create a pocket so you don't have to cut the full blade width. Always use test boards with each new saw setup to check cutting depths and fence settings before making passes on project pieces.

Extend the miter gauge for making more accurate crosscuts by screwing a 1x3 through the mounting holes. (Select screw lengths that won't penetrate the front of the board.) Clamp a stop block to the 1x3 for making multiple identical cuts (Photo 3).

Measure and scribe as you go

When you're building cabinets, it's important to remeasure as the cabinet takes shape. For example, once you dry-fit the box (piecing it together before assembly), take new measurements for the plywood back. Use the back to square up the cabinet before the glue sets up. Similarly, first dry-fit the door rails and stiles together to size the plywood panel for the door. Use a thin ruler inside the

frame dadoes and subtract about 1/8 in. in both dimensions to allow for expansion. Check the lengths of the cleats, hanging rail and top and bottom trim before cutting them, too.

Sneaking up on cuts

You don't have to strive to set up the saw to make it cut perfect dadoes and rabbets on the first pass. Just remember to leave depths and widths a little on the short side. You can always crank up the blade or move the fence slightly and make second and third passes until widths and depths are perfect.

Flipping boards end for end and making a second pass will precisely center the dadoes for the door panel (Photo 9). You can simply eyeball the blade to center it in the door frame parts. After you make the first pass, flip the door frame parts end for end and send them through again. That'll center the dado perfectly. Test-fit the 1/4-in. plywood for a smooth fit without forcing it. If it's a little tight, move the fence very slightly away from the blade and repeat the same two passes. Continue until the plywood slips snugly into the groove.

Center the tenons in the door rails (the top and bottom door frame boards) with a similar flipping technique (Photo 10). Set the dado blade slightly less than 5/16 in. above the saw table, make a pass, then flip over the board and make the same pass on the other side. Check the fit in the grooves of the stiles—the vertical door frame boards (Photo 11). Raise the blade slightly and repeat the steps until the tenon fits snugly.

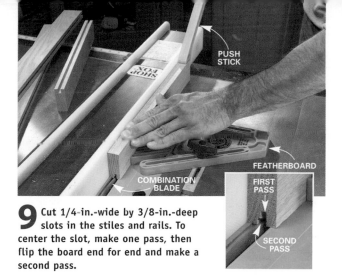

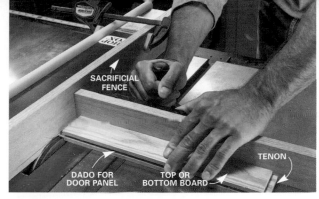

9 Cut 1/4-in.-wide by 3/8-in.-deep slots in the stiles and rails. To center the slot, make one pass, then flip the board end for end and make a second pass.

10 Set the dado blade at 5/16 in. above the saw table and 5/16 in. away from the fence. Cut the tenons at both ends of the door frame rails. Check the fit. Adjust width and depth and recut until the tenon fits the door panel dado snugly.

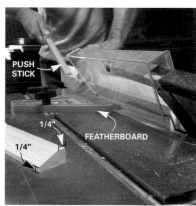

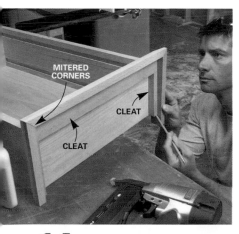

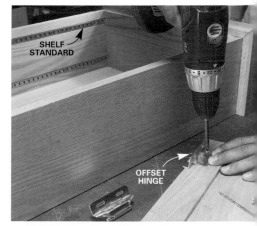

11 Dry-fit the door parts, then smear a little glue on the tenons and assemble. Clamp the door frame together until the glue sets.

12 Set the saw and combination blade to rip at a 25-degree bevel. Rip the bevels on the top trim pieces. Sand out the saw marks.

13 Cut the miters using the miter gauge set to exactly 90 degrees and the saw blade set at a 45-degree bevel.

14 Glue and nail on the top cleats as shown in Figure A. Fit the miters, then glue and nail the top trim to the cleats.

15 Glue and nail on the bottom cleats (Figure A). Then glue on the bottom trim and nail it with 1-1/2-in. brads.

16 Screw the shelf standards into the dadoes. Screw the hinges to the door (Figure A), then center the door and screw the hinges to the cabinet.

Sanding and finishing

You'll have some sanding to do, particularly on the ripped edges. Sand out saw marks prior to any assembly. Start with 100-grit sandpaper and then work your way through 120- and 150-grit paper. Be careful not to round any edges where joints meet or you'll have little cracks that'll show. Ease sharp edges with 150-grit paper after assembly to "soften" the cabinet. Factory edges and surfaces should also be lightly sanded with 150-grit paper prior to finishing.

Mount the shelf standards, hinges and knob on the cabinet, but remove them prior to finishing. That'll make the job easier, and keep finish off the hardware.

21 Closet nook shelves

Salvage the hidden space at the recessed ends of your closets by adding a set of shelves. Wire shelves are available in a variety of widths. Measure the width and depth of the space. Then choose the correct shelving and ask the salesperson to cut the shelves to length for you. Subtract 3/8 in. from the actual width to determine the shelf length. Buy a pair of end mounting brackets and a pair of plastic clips for each shelf.

Make the most of the recesses at the ends of your closet with wire shelving.

22 On-a-roll pegboard doors

SLIDING DOORS

3/4" PLYWOOD TOP, BOTTOM, AND SIDES

SLIDING DOOR HARDWARE

1/2" PLYWOOD SPACER

2" BETWEEN DOORS

FLOOR BRACKET

Maximize hand tool storage in a tool cabinet with these slick doors. The key to this project is a 4-ft.-long By-Pass Sliding Door Hardware Set ($11 at a home center). Mount 1/4-in. pegboard onto it, making sure to provide enough room (2 in.) to hang tools on the pegboard and still allow it to slide by the door in front. The trick is to insert 1/2-in. plywood spacers in the roller hardware as shown. You can use the floor bracket that comes with the slider hardware to maintain the same 2-in. clearance at the bottom of the cabinet. For door handles, simply drill a couple of 1-1/4-in. holes in the pegboard with a spade bit. Now pop in the pegs and hang up your tools.

23 Reverse-osmosis water filter system

If you buy lots of bottled or filtered water or you're worried about your tap water, a reverse-osmosis water filter can be a good investment. For $150 to $300, it can provide 10 or more gallons of drinking water a day. Replacement filters will cost $100 to $200 annually.

Reverse-osmosis filters remove many pollutants and chemicals, separating them from the water and then flushing them into the drain line. The purified water is then fed to the storage tank or the spout on the sink. However, reverse-osmosis filters remove the minerals like calcium and magnesium that give water its taste, so try a gallon (available at most supermarkets) before buying a system.

First, hang the filter assembly on the back or side wall of the sink base (or in the basement close to the sink location) at the height specified in the instructions. Turn off both the cold and the hot water shutoffs, and then install (after the cold water shutoff) the tee or saddle valve included with the unit.

Cut the color-coded water supply line so that it's above the cabinet base and won't get kinked. Fasten the plastic tubing to the supply valve (Photo 1).

Shorten the supply and waste lines to the faucet to eliminate excess tubing, but don't cut the larger black waste line yet. Attach the lines to the fittings on the base of the faucet (Photo 2). The black waste lines feed through the base of the faucet to keep them above possible sink backups, but they have no connection to the supply.

Fasten the faucet to the sink, then install the drain-line adapter under the sink basket. Cut the waste line so that it flows downhill with no loops, then push it into the adapter (Photo 3).

Set the storage tank into place and install the final water line. Sterilize and fill the system according to the manufacturer's instructions (Photo 4).

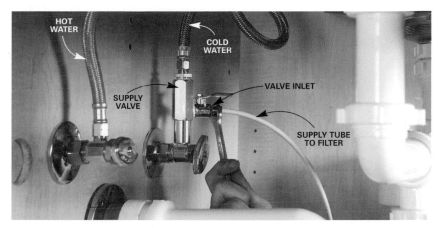

1 Push the plastic supply tube onto the supply valve, then tighten the nut a half turn past hand tight.

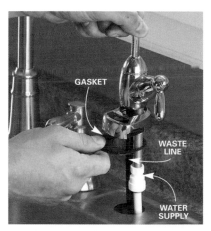

2 Feed the water supply line and the two waste lines up through the hole in the sink and through the gasket and faucet base, then attach them.

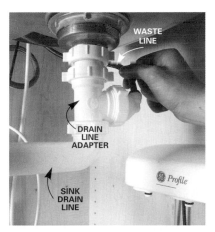

3 Install the drain line adapter just below the sink and above the discharge from the disposer and/or dishwasher.

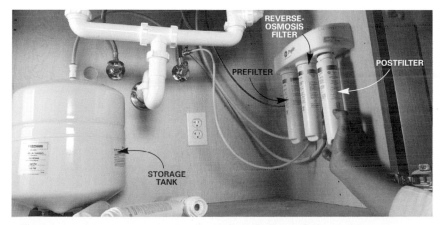

4 Before using the system, sanitize it and then fill and drain it to rinse it clean. Check all the fittings for leaks.

24 Turned pen holder

STEP OFF HOLE CENTERS

SAME SETTING

THREE SHIMS

Make one of these and get ready to fill gift orders! On a lathe, turn a 3-in.-square x 6-in.-long hardwood blank into a cylinder that's 4-1/2 in. long with a narrowed waist, curved top and flat bottom. Sand smooth. With a compass, draw a circle on the top and mark six hole locations on the circle. Why six? When you leave the compass at the same radius and "step" it around the circle, it marks off six equally spaced points. After marking, use a 3/8-in. brad point bit to drill the six holes at 10 degrees and 2 in. deep. If your drill press has no angle adjustment, glue three shims together and clamp them to the table to make a 10-degree angled ramp. Finish the pen holder with Danish oil, and load with pens.

25 Shop stool/stepladder

Here's a double-duty project you'll wonder how you lived without. It's a solid, comfortable stool, and when you flip over the hinged seat board, it becomes a stepladder.

Assemble the two sides first. Drill pilot holes, countersink and attach the leg braces to the legs with 1-1/4-in. drywall screws and wood glue. Screw the top leg brace flush with the top of the legs, and the lower braces 8-1/2 in. and 16-3/4 in. up from the lower ends of the legs. Attach the step boards and the back brace with 2-in. drywall screws and glue. Round over the top outside edges of the seat boards with a 1/4-in. round-over bit. Connect the seat boards with two 2-in.-wide butt hinges, and fasten the rear seat board to the top leg brace with 2-in. drywall screws and glue.

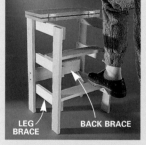

LEG BRACE   BACK BRACE

Cutting list
1x4 Pine: 4 legs, 25 in. long; 6 leg braces, 14 in. long; 2 steps and 1 back brace, 16 in. long
1x8 Pine: 2 seat boards, 18 in. long x 7-1/4 in. wide

26 Petite shelves

CUT DADOES BEFORE RIPPING LEGS

BEVEL LOWER SHELF EDGES

BRASS SCREWS AND FINISH WASHERS

Turn a single 3-ft.-long, 1x12 hardwood board into some small shelves to organize a desktop or counter. Cut off a 21-in.-long board for the shelves, rip it in the middle to make two shelves, and cut 45-degree bevels on the two long front edges with a router or table saw. Bevel the ends of the other board, cut dadoes, which are grooves cut into the wood with a router or a table saw with a dado blade, crosswise (cut a dado on scrap and test-fit the shelves first!) and rip it into four narrower boards, two at 1-3/8 in. wide and two at 4 in. Finish, then assemble with brass screws and finish washers.

27 Sliding bookend

To corral shelf-dwelling books or CDs that like to wander, cut 3/4-in.-thick hardwood pieces into 6-in. x 6-in. squares. Use a band saw or jigsaw to cut a slot along one edge (with the grain) that's a smidgen wider than the shelf thickness. Stop the notch 3/4 in. from the other edge. Finish the bookend and slide it on the shelf.

28 Easy-to-build knife block

Display your kitchen cutlery in style with this handsome knife block. It's fast, easy and fun to build, and includes a 6-in.-wide storage box for a knife sharpener. The Accusharp knife sharpener ($11, product No. 001, www.accusharp.com) tucks neatly inside.

To build one, you only need a 3/4-in. x 8-in. x 4-ft. hardwood board and a 6-in. x 6-1/2-in. piece of 1/4-in. hardwood plywood to match.

Begin by cutting off a 10-in. length of the board and setting it aside. Rip the remaining 38-in. board to 6 in. wide and cut five evenly spaced saw kerfs 5/8 in. deep along one face. Crosscut the slotted board into four 9-in. pieces and glue them into a block, being careful not to slop glue into the saw kerfs (you can clean them out with a knife before the glue dries). Saw a 15-degree angle on one end and screw the plywood piece under the angled end of the block.

Cut the 6-1/2-in. x 3-1/2-in. lid from the leftover board, and slice the remaining piece into 1/4-in.-thick pieces for the sides and end of the box. Glue them around the plywood floor. Cut a rabbet, which is a groove cut into the edge of the wood, on three sides of the lid so it fits snugly on the box and drill a 5/8-in. hole for a finger pull. Then just add a finish.

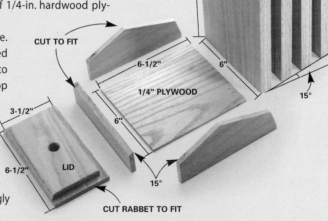

5/8"DEEP
9"
CUT TO FIT
6-1/2"
6"
1/4" PLYWOOD
6"
15°
3-1/2"
6-1/2"
LID
15°
CUT RABBET TO FIT

29 Swedish boot scraper

Here's a traditional Swedish farm accessory for gunk-laden soles. The dimensions are not critical, but be sure the edges of the slats are fairly sharp—they're what makes the boot scraper work. Cut slats to length, then cut triangular openings on the side of a pair of 2x2s. A radial arm saw works well for this, but a table saw or band saw will also make the cut. Trim the 2x2s to length, predrill, and use galvanized screws to attach the slats from underneath.

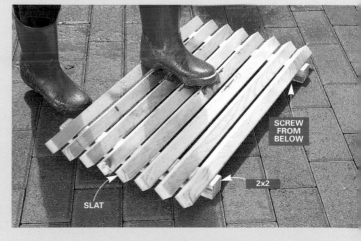

SCREW FROM BELOW

2x2

SLAT

30 Better bagel slicer

This bagel slicer is as easy to build as it is to use. Making it requires only a few simple tools, two dowels and a scrap of hardwood. When your stomach growls, drop the bagel in the cage, squeeze the dowel tops so the side dowels bend and pinch the bagel, then slice away. It keeps your fingers out of harm's way (and the crumbs and knife blade off your counter).

Dowel diameters vary slightly. To ensure you get a good fit, drill a sample hole with your 3/16-in. brad point bit and take that scrap with you to test-fit the 3/16-in. dowels you buy.

Use mineral oil (available at drug stores) to finish your bagel slicer. It's nontoxic dry or wet. (If you decide to use a different finish, be sure it's nontoxic when dry.)

Build the bagel slicer

Cut the dowels and hardwood base to the dimensions in the Cutting list on p. 43.

Lay out the holes in the base (Figure A). Make a drill guide by cutting a 5-degree angle on the end of a piece of scrap wood, then use it to guide your bit as you drill (Photo 1). Use a 2-in.-high guide and let the bit protrude 2-3/8 in. beyond the chuck. With this setup, when the chuck meets the top of the guide you'll get uniform 3/8-in.-deep holes.

Lay out the holes in the handles. Hold each in a vise or clamp while drilling the holes. Wrap a piece of masking tape 3/8 in. from the tip of your bit to act as a depth guide.

Glue and tap the uprights into the handles. Be careful not to damage the ends of the uprights that fit into the base. Then glue and tap the uprights into the base (Photo 2).

Let the glue dry, ease all the sharp edges with sandpaper, then apply a coat of mineral oil for the finish (Photo 3). Let the finish dry overnight and you're ready for breakfast.

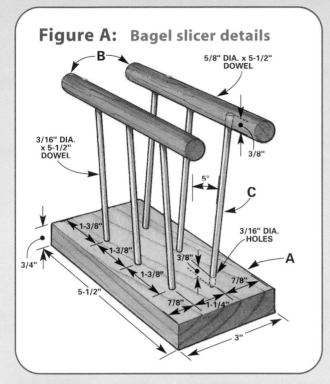

Figure A: Bagel slicer details

B

5/8" DIA. x 5-1/2" DOWEL

3/16" DIA. x 5-1/2" DOWEL

3/8"

5°

C

1-3/8"

1-3/8"

3/16" DIA. HOLES

3/8"

A

1-3/8"

3/4"

7/8"

5-1/2"

7/8"

1-1/4"

3"

5° ANGLE

3/16" DIA. BRAD POINT BIT

2-3/8"

2"

ANGLE-DRILLING GUIDE

3/8" DEEP HOLES

1 Drill the angled holes in the base. Guide the bit against the end of a 2-in.-wide piece of scrap wood with a 5-degree angle cut on the end. Set the bit in the chuck at a depth so that when the chuck hits the guide block, the hole is 3/8 in. deep.

WOOD GLUE

RUBBER MALLET

2 Tap the preassembled dowel sides into the base using a rubber mallet. Start by inserting one of the end dowels, then work your way down to the other end. Glue all joints.

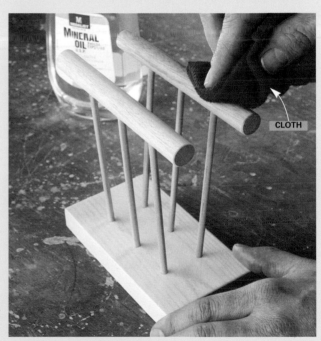

CLOTH

3 Wipe on a coat of mineral oil to finish the wood.

Materials list

3/4" x 3" x 5-1/2" birch

5/8" dia. x 12" hardwood dowel

3/16" dia. x 36" hardwood dowel

Small bottle of mineral oil

Cutting list

Key	Pcs.	Size & description
A	1	3/4" x 3" x 5-1/2" birch (base)
B	2	5/8" dia. x 5-1/2" hardwood dowel (handles)
C	6	3/16" dia. x 5-1/2" hardwood dowel (uprights)

31 Butterfly house

Butterflies like the protection of dark, sheltered areas—whether it's for months at a time (during long, cold winters), or for just a few moments (when dodging hungry predators). Here's a simple refuge you can build for them for under $20.

Use smooth or rough-sawn cedar; it's rot-resistant and weathers to a mellow gray. For durability, assemble the house using moisture-proof glue and galvanized nails. Make sure to hinge and latch one side so you can insert and maintain the long twigs and tree bark the butterflies roost on (Figure A, p. 45).

A jigsaw, drill and common hand tools are all you need, although a table saw (to cut angles and the wood to size) speeds up the work greatly.

To attract butterflies, locate the house in an area with lots of flowering plants, and mount it 2 to 3 ft. off the ground.

Build the butterfly house

Cut the parts to the sizes and angles listed in the Cutting list, p. 45 and shown in the photos.

Lay out the entry slots on the front (Figure A), drill the ends with a 3/8-in.-dia. bit, then cut the slots the rest of the way with a jigsaw (Photo 1). Smooth the sides of the slots with sandpaper.

Use a 7/8-in. spade bit to drill the holes for the support pipe in the bottom, and one of the pipe stops.

Glue and nail the back to the side. Glue and clamp the two support pipe stops together, then glue and clamp them to the back. Glue and nail the bottom to the assembled back and side.

Glue and nail the false front roof pieces to the front, then glue and nail the front in place, and attach the roof boards. Use the door as a spacer between the front and back when you attach the roof.

Trim the door, if necessary, so it fits loosely between the front and back. Align the door, and hammer in the two hinge pivot nails (Photo 2).

Use two pliers to bend a nail in half. Drill a pilot hole, then tap in this latch.

Insert the support pipe through the bottom and into the pipe stop. Drill pilot holes for the pipe strap screws, attach the strap (Photo 3), then loosen it and remove the support pipe.

Determine the best location and height for the house (keep it low). Hammer the pipe into the ground (protect the end of the pipe with a scrap piece of wood), then slide the house on the pipe, tighten the pipe strap, and watch for your first fluttering houseguests.

JIGSAW

3/8" DIA. STARTER HOLES

1 Create the entry slots. Drill 3/8-in. holes for the top and bottom of each slot, then connect the holes using a jigsaw.

To attract butterflies, locate the house in an area with lots of flowering plants.

Materials list

Item	Qty.
1x6 x 10' cedar	1
4d galvanized casing nails	25
3/4" dia. type L copper pipe*	1
3/4" copper pipe strap*	1
No. 8 x 1/2" pan head screws	2
Titebond II moisture-proof glue	small bottle

*Available at home centers

Cutting list

Key	Pcs.	Size & description
A	2	3/4" x 5" x 24" cedar (front and back)
B	2	3/4" x 5" x 6-1/4" cedar (roof boards)
C	2	3/4" x 3-3/4" x 22-1/4" cedar (side and door)
D	1	3/4" x 3-3/4" x 3-1/2" cedar (bottom)
E	2	3/4" x 1-1/4" x 3-1/2" cedar (support pipe stop)
F	2	1/2" x 3/4" x 3-1/2" cedar (false front roof)

Figure A: Butterfly house

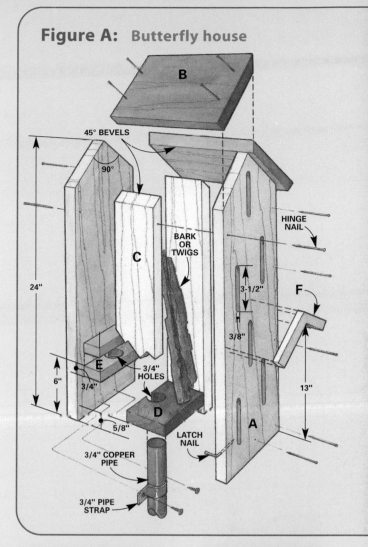

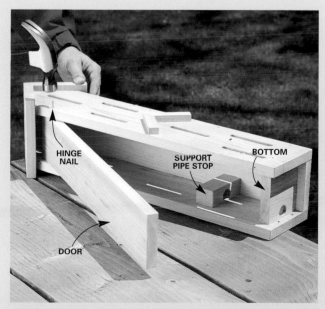

2 Assemble the house. Use straight nails for the door hinges and a bent one for the latch. (Note: Here the door is open so you can see the inside, but it's easier to align everything with the door closed.)

3 Loosely screw the pipe strap to the back, using the support pipe as a guide. Remove the pipe, pound it into the ground, then permanently tighten the strap around the pipe to prevent the house from spinning.

32 Portable bookshelf

Here's a cool knockdown shelf for a dorm room or den. You just slide the shelves between the dowels, and they pinch the shelves to stiffen the bookshelf. It works great if you're careful about two things: Make the space between the dowel holes exactly 1/16 in. wider than the thickness of the shelf board. And be sure the shelf thickness is the same from end to end and side to side.

After test-fitting a dowel in a trial hole (you want a tight fit), drill holes in a jig board so the space between the holes is your shelf thickness plus 1/16 in. Clamp the jig board on the ends of the legs and drill the holes. Cut the dowels 1-3/4 in. longer than the shelf width, then dry-assemble (no

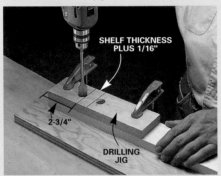

SHELF THICKNESS PLUS 1/16"
2-3/4"
DRILLING JIG

glue). Mark the angled ends of the legs parallel to the shelves and cut off the tips to make the legs sit flat. Disassemble and glue the dowels in the leg holes. When the glue dries, slide the shelves in and load them up.

Cutting list
Perfectly flat 1x12 lumber or plywood
2 shelves: 11-1/4" wide x 3' long
4 risers: 2-1/4" wide x 24" long
8 dowels: 3/4" dia. x 13" long

33 Simple stepstool

Here's a great gift idea that will draw raves. The joints are accurately made in seconds with a plate jointer, but don't tell your admirers. You'll also need a miter saw to crosscut the boards and a jigsaw to cut the half-circles in the risers. The lumber you'll need:

■ One 8-ft. 1x8 clear hardwood board (actual width is 7-1/4 in. and actual thickness is 3/4 in.). Oak is a good choice because it's readily available at home centers.
■ One 3-ft. 1x3 hardwood board (actual width is 2-1/2 in. and actual thickness is 3/4 in.).

Cut the 8-ft. board into:
■ Two 22-in. riser boards   ■ One 14-in. step board
■ Two 11-in. riser boards   ■ One 14-in. seat board

You'll use 94 in. of the 96-in. board, so make practice cuts on a scrap board first to check the angle and length of cut. Don't cut the 3-ft. 1x3 board until you've dry-assembled the step, seat and risers and measured for a perfect fit.

To create two risers, join the 11-in. boards to the 22-in. boards with No. 20 biscuits and glue. Let dry 30 minutes, then lay the step and seat across and

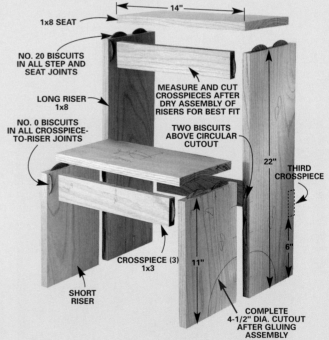

14"
1x8 SEAT
NO. 20 BISCUITS IN ALL STEP AND SEAT JOINTS
LONG RISER 1x8
NO. 0 BISCUITS IN ALL CROSSPIECE-TO-RISER JOINTS
MEASURE AND CUT CROSSPIECES AFTER DRY ASSEMBLY OF RISERS FOR BEST FIT
TWO BISCUITS ABOVE CIRCULAR CUTOUT
22"
THIRD CROSSPIECE
6"
CROSSPIECE (3) 1x3
11"
SHORT RISER
COMPLETE 4-1/2" DIA. CUTOUT AFTER GLUING ASSEMBLY

mark for two No. 20 biscuits at each joint. Dry-assemble the step, seat and risers with biscuits, then cut and snugly fit the crosspieces. Mark the riser-to-crosspiece joint and cut slots for No. 0 biscuits. Glue and firmly clamp the step, seat and crosspieces to the risers. Check for square and let dry 30 minutes, then cut out the 4-1/2-in.-diameter arc on the bottom of the risers to create the legs. Finish-sand and apply your favorite finish. This project is designed for use on hard-surface flooring only—not carpeting.

This chapter will walk you through fixes for all those annoying problems around the house. You'll find help for everything from running toilets to cracks in your walls and brown spots in your yard.

Chapter 2

home repairs

Stop a **running toilet**

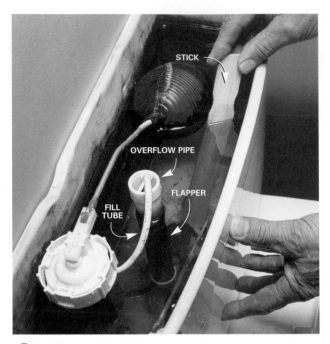

1 Push down on the flapper with a stick when you hear the water running and listen for it to stop. If it stops, you know the flapper isn't sealing properly. Replace it. Check the fill tube length and cut it back so it's at least 1/2 in. above the water line.

The mysteries of a running toilet can drive you nuts. Whether you hear water running constantly or cycling on and off, read on to learn how to stop most leaks. Hardware stores and home centers carry the parts for almost every repair.

One cause of a running toilet is a flapper that doesn't seal. If water from the tank seeps around the flapper and into the bowl, the flapper is probably shot. Test for a leaky flapper as shown in Photo 1.

To replace the flapper, first shut off the water supply valve under the toilet (or the main supply if the valve leaks!). Flush the toilet to drain out most of the water, and unhook the old flapper. Buy a new flapper of the same type and install it according to the instructions on the package. Hook the flapper chain onto the flush lever arm so there's a little slack when the flapper is closed.

If the flapper doesn't leak and the water still runs, inspect the fill tube connected to the overflow pipe (Photo 1). The end should be above the water line. If the end is under water, cut it back.

Next, inspect the fill valve for visible signs of wear and test the float (Photo 2). If the float is improperly adjusted, the tank water level can rise above the overflow pipe and drain into it. Replace the old fill valve if it doesn't completely shut off or it hampers the float-arm operation (Photo 3).

Install a new "floatcup"-style fill valve as shown in Photos 4 and 5. Adjust the float according to the package instructions to

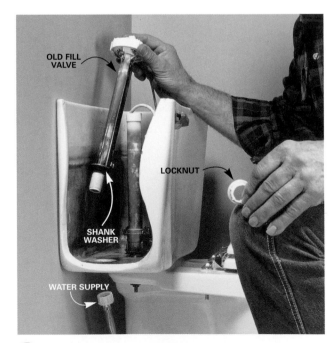

2 Flush the toilet and look for a fill valve leak. Lift up on the float arm when the tank is filling to see if the water stops. Bend or adjust the float arm so the tank stops filling when the water level is 1/2 to 1 in. below the top of the overflow pipe. If the fill valve still leaks, replace it (Photo 3).

3 Turn off the water supply, flush the toilet and sponge the remaining water from the tank. Disconnect the water supply line, unscrew the fill valve locknut and lift out the old fill valve.

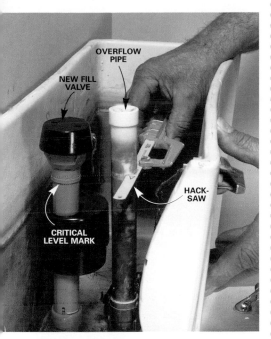

OVERFLOW PIPE

NEW FILL VALVE

HACK-SAW

CRITICAL LEVEL MARK

4 Insert the new fill valve into the tank and tighten the locknut a half turn past hand-tight. If the fill valve is at its maximum height, but the overflow pipe is still higher than the critical level mark, shorten the overflow pipe with a hacksaw so it's 1 in. lower than the critical level mark on the fill valve.

establish the proper water level. Finish the installation by attaching the flapper chain to the flush lever. Turn on the water and test flush the toilet.

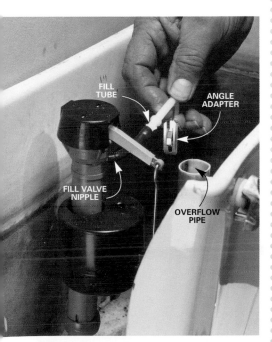

FILL TUBE

ANGLE ADAPTER

FILL VALVE NIPPLE

OVERFLOW PIPE

5 Attach one end of the new fill tube to the fill valve nipple and the other to the enclosed angle adapter (shorten the tube to avoid kinks, if necessary). Clip the angle adapter onto the overflow pipe.

35 Install toggle bolts

Fastening towel bars, shelves or hooks to a fiberglass or plastic shower surround can be tricky. The surround is simply too thin to hold screws and there's often a gap of 1 in. or more between the surround and the wall studs behind it. But with 1/8-in. toggle bolts, you can mount most light-duty hardware (like the adjustable showerhead bar shown here). Keep in mind that this leaves big holes (3/8 in.) in the surround that can't be patched later, so anything you mount will have to stay there permanently. The mounting system shown here isn't strong enough to support the full weight of a person, so we don't recommend it for installing safety grab bars.

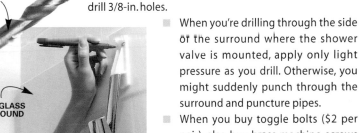

STEEL SCREW

BRASS SCREW

TOGGLE

Everything you need is available at home centers and hardware stores. Here are some pointers:

■ Some areas of a fiberglass surround may be reinforced with plywood. After you mark the hole locations (Photo 1), drill 3/16-in. holes. If you strike plywood behind the fiberglass, you can drive in stainless steel screws instead of using toggle bolts. If you don't hit plywood, drill 3/8-in. holes.

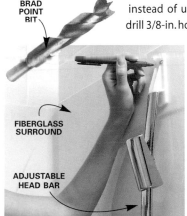

BRAD POINT BIT

FIBERGLASS SURROUND

ADJUSTABLE HEAD BAR

1 Mark the hole positions and drill 3/8-in. holes through the fiberglass. For a clean, chip-free hole, use a brad point bit.

■ When you're drilling through the side of the surround where the shower valve is mounted, apply only light pressure as you drill. Otherwise, you might suddenly punch through the surround and puncture pipes.

■ When you buy toggle bolts ($2 per pair), also buy brass machine screws ($1) to replace the steel screws that come with the toggles. Steel heads will rust and stain the surround.

■ When you tighten the toggle bolts (Photo 3), it's OK to use a drill. But do the final tightening by hand. Too much torque can crack the surround.

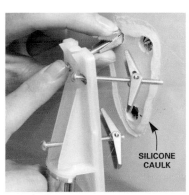

SILICONE CAULK

2 Run a light bead of silicone caulk around the holes and insert the toggle bolts.

3 Tighten the toggle bolts. Hold the mounting bracket away from the wall as you turn the screws; otherwise the toggle will simply spin inside the wall.

36 Adjust a dragging shower door

If the sliding doors on your shower or bathtub don't glide smoothly, repair them soon. A door that drags on the lower track will eventually do permanent damage to both the door and the track. A dragging roller at the top of the door will wear and require replacement.

To start, make sure the rollers on both doors are riding on the tracks inside the upper rail. Sometimes, one roller falls out of the track and the bottom edge of the door skids along the lower rail. In that case, you only have to lift the door and guide the roller back onto the track.

If an off-track roller isn't the problem, you'll have to remove the doors to adjust and possibly replace the rollers. Many doors have a small plastic guide at the middle of the lower rail. To remove this type of guide, just remove a single screw. Others have a guide rail screwed to the door (Photo 1).

With the guide removed, lift the doors out of their tracks (Photo 2). Then make sure the rollers turn easily. If not, apply a little silicone spray lubricant. Some lubricants can

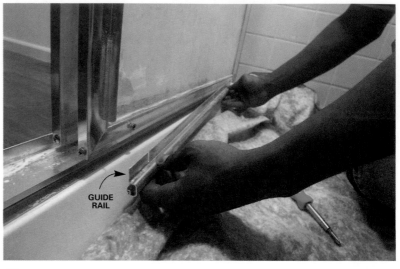

1 Unscrew the guide at the lower edge of the sliding door. Protect the shower or tub from scratches with a drop cloth.

harm plastic, so check the label. If the lubricant doesn't do the trick, replace the rollers. Most home centers and some hardware stores carry replacements ($3 per pair). Take an old roller with you to find a match. In many cases, you can use a replacement that's slightly larger or smaller than the original. But be sure to check that the original and replacement edges match—either rounded or flat. If you can't find rollers locally, type "shower door parts" into any online search engine to find a supplier.

Screw the new rollers into place and rehang the doors. You'll probably have to remove the doors once or twice to adjust the rollers for smooth operation (Photo 3).

 ROUND EDGE  FLAT EDGE

2 Lift the door out of its track inside the upper rail. Tilt each door in or out to remove it. Wipe both tracks clean.

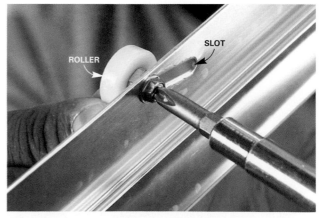

3 Raise or lower each door by repositioning the roller in its slanted slot. Loosen the screw to move the roller.

37 Sharpen your mower blade

One of the best ways to encourage a greener, fuller and healthier lawn is to sharpen your lawn mower blade. A dull blade rips and pulls the grass blades, leaving ragged tears that both weaken the plant and promote fungal growth and other grass diseases. A sharp blade, on the other hand, cuts cleanly, allowing the plant to heal and recover quickly. Sharp blades also let you complete your lawn-cutting chore faster and with less stress on the mower.

Sharpening is a simple task, even for a novice. It'll take a few sharpenings to master the technique. After that, the chore will take less than 10 minutes. Plan to do it twice every mowing season. Here you'll learn the steps that will work for just about any walk-behind mower.

Play it safe when removing the blade

Always disconnect the spark plug wire and remove the spark plug before you touch the blade (Photo 1). The blade and shaft are directly connected to the motor, and in some cases turning the blade by hand could cause the motor to fire, unless the spark plug is removed.

Then look for the carburetor and air filter. The carburetor is usually easy to recognize because it has throttle cables running to it. If you keep this side up when you tip your mower over to get at the blade (Photo 2), you won't get a smoke cloud from leaking oil the next time you start it. Some mowers have gas caps with air holes that could leak a little gas onto your garage floor, so work outside or keep a rag handy to clean up drips. Once the blade is off, set the mower back onto all four wheels until you're ready to reinstall your blade.

You'll usually find a single bolt or nut holding the blade on. It's usually very tight and you'll need to clamp the blade to loosen it. The 2x4 method shown here (Photo 3) is simple, quick and safe.

1 Pull the spark plug wire from the spark plug to prevent the motor from accidentally starting. Then remove the spark plug.

2 Turn the mower onto its side with the air filter and carburetor side up. This keeps oil and gas from dripping into the air filter.

AIR FILTER

Mark your blade

Mark your blade with spray paint before you remove it so you know which way to reinstall it. Mower repair pros say that the biggest mistake homeowners make is installing a blade upside down after sharpening it. The blade won't cut—and they'll go nuts trying to figure out why!

SPRAY PAINT

BREAKER BAR WITH SOCKET

BLADE WEDGE

3 Wedge a short 2x4 between the blade and the deck to clamp the blade. Loosen the bolt (or nut) with a long-handled wrench. Turn counterclockwise. Remove the bolt and blade.

Don't use your foot! A good tool to keep handy to loosen the bolt is a 10-in. breaker bar with a socket to match the bolt. It'll give you plenty of leverage to loosen extremely tight bolts, and you can keep your knuckles well away from the blade when bearing down. Use a squirt of penetrating oil on really rusted, stuck bolts. Wait 10 minutes to give it time to work.

Sharpen it with a file

Sharpen the blade with a hand file (Photo 4). Mower blades are made from fairly soft steel. You can sharpen most blades with fewer than 50 strokes of a clean, sharp mill bastard file that's at least 10 in. long. Grinders also work, and much more quickly. (Pros use them.) But they're more difficult to control and you might overheat and ruin the blade.

Always sharpen from the top side of the cutting edge; this will give you the longest-lasting edge on the blade. The file cuts in one direction only, on the push stroke; you'll feel it bite into the steel on the blade. If you don't feel that cutting action, your file is probably dull or you're not pressing down hard enough. Don't try to make your blade razor sharp; it'll dull more quickly. "Butter knife" sharp will do.

Sharpening mulching blades is sometimes more difficult. Mulching blades may have longer or curved cutting edges, and you may need several types of files to sharpen them. In some cases, you may have to resort to a 4-1/2-in. angle grinder. If your blade is too difficult to sharpen, take it to a hardware store or a blade sharpening service. You can have it sharpened for about $6.

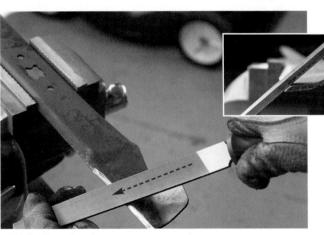

ORIGINAL CUTTING ANGLE

4 Clamp the blade in a vise and sharpen the cutting edge with a mill bastard file, held at the same cutting angle as before. File until the blade is "butter knife" sharp.

✳ Do you need a new blade?

Examine your blade when you remove it and look for the problems shown here. If you're unsure of the condition of the blade, take it to a hardware store or home center and compare it with a new one.

BENT
Set your old blade on your workbench and check for bends. If you're unsure, compare it with a new blade.

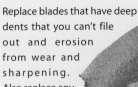

NEW BLADE

DENTS IN CUTTING EDGE
Replace blades that have deep dents that you can't file out and erosion from wear and sharpening. Also replace any blade that has cracked.

CUTTING EDGE

5 Hang the blade on a nail to check the balance. If one side dips, file a bit more off that side until the blade remains horizontal.

NAIL

Balance it before reinstalling

Before you reinstall the blade, be sure to balance it. An unbalanced blade will cause vibration and possibly ruin the blade shaft or bearings. To check the balance, simply drive a nail into a stud and set the blade onto it like an airplane propeller (Photo 5). If one side falls, it's heavier, and you have to file more metal off it. Keep filing until the blade stays level.

Reinstall the blade and hand-tighten the bolt. Insert the 2x4 in the reverse direction so you can bear down on the breaker bar to tighten the bolt. It's difficult to overtighten the bolt. Mower sharpening pros say that the second most common mistake they see is undertightening the bolt. A loose blade throws off the engine timing and sometimes makes the mower hard to start.

6 Reinstall the blade and screw in the bolt. Then wedge the 2x4 back in and tighten the bolt firmly with your socket and breaker bar.

No excuses!

To get in the habit of keeping your blade sharp, dedicate a set of tools for sharpening only. Hang them nearby so they're ready to go. And keep a second, sharp blade handy too. You can slip it on and sharpen the dull one later.

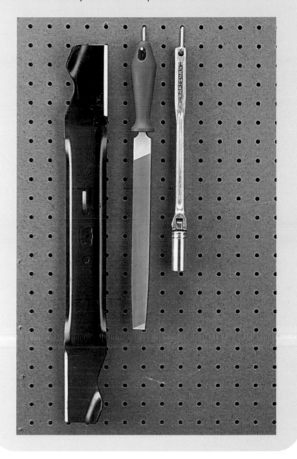

Buying a new blade

Always replace your blade with an exact replacement blade, or the blade recommended in your owner's manual. Resist the temptation to convert your regular straight-blade mower to a fancier mulching mower by simply changing the blade. Your mower probably won't work any differently than before, and it may not work as well. The mower deck on a straight-blade mower is shallow and has a side discharge to eject the grass clippings quickly. A mulching mower has a deeper deck without a side discharge; the grass is chopped three or four times before it drops to the ground. The mower design is as important as the blade.

REGULAR BLADE

MULCHING BLADE

THIN TRAILING EDGE

The trailing edge, or fin, is the edge opposite the cutting edge. This fin is often slanted upward, which creates an updraft to lift the grass and grass clippings. Dust and sand will wear this fin down. When it's thin, replace the blade.

NEW BLADE

OLD BLADE

THICK TRAILING EDGE

THIN TRAILING EDGE

38 Give your lawn first aid

Problem: Dog spots on grass

Symptoms: Dog spots are round patches about 4 to 8 in. in diameter with dead grass in the middle, encircled by dark green grass. They're most apparent in the early spring when dormant grass first begins to turn green again.

Cause: Dog urine contains high concentrations of acids, salts and nitrogen, which burn (dry out) the grass roots and kill them. As rain washes the area, the urine is diluted and the nitrogen spreads, causing the grass surrounding the spot to grow faster and turn greener.

Remedy: You have to replant your grass; it won't come back on its own. But first you have to dilute or remove the caustic urine from the soil (Photo 1).

tip When you're watering new seed, moisten the soil daily and keep it damp—but don't soak it. Overwatering is a common mistake.

An ounce of prevention

1. Soak your pet's favorite areas in your lawn to get the salts out of the root zone before they kill the grass.
2. Fertilize your lawn in the spring to boost the overall color and mask the darker green dog spots.
3. Train your pet to urinate in a designated area. Replace or repair the grass in this area annually or cover it with mulch.
4. Keep your pet well hydrated to make its urine less concentrated.

Thoroughly soak the area with lots of water. Let the hose run for at least three minutes. Then you can start the replanting process (Photo 2). Add a half inch of new soil to help absorb any remaining urine (Photo 3). Then you can spread new seed or use a commercial yard patch mixture (available at most nurseries or home centers) or even sod. In any case, the secret of good germination is keeping the seed moist. And keep the area moist until the new grass is about 3 in. high.

Recovery time: Four to six weeks

1 Soak the patch until the grass is sopping wet to dilute the urine acids and salts and wash them deeper into the soil, beyond the grass roots.

2 Scrape up the dead grass with a hand rake and remove it. Rough up the area to loosen the soil 1/2 in. deep. Seeds germinate better in soft soil.

3 Sprinkle on a 1/2-in.-thick layer of topsoil, then pepper it with grass seed. Cover with a pinch of new soil and press it to firm it up. Keep the area moist until the new grass is about 3 in. high.

Problem: Grubs

Symptoms: Grub-chewed turf has patchy areas that wilt and die. You can easily pull up the affected turf if you tug on it. Another indicator of grubs may be increased raccoon, bird or mole activity. They like to dig up and eat the grubs at night. While this may sound good, the moles will kill the grass as they forage for grubs.

Cause: Lawn grubs are the larval stage of moths and beetles. The grubs eat the roots of grass, which causes death by dehydration.

Remedy: Be vigilant. Are beetles swarming around your porch light? In the next month, keep an eye out for patches of grass that wilt or are blue-green on hot days. They may be larvae infested. Turn over some turf (Photo 1). If you count six to 10 grubs (white wormlike larvae with black heads) under a 1-ft.-square area of sod, consider using a grub insecticide (available at home centers and nurseries). Or talk to a professional (look under "Grass Service" in your yellow pages) about treating your yard. They will be familiar with the grub problems in your region and the most suitable treatment methods.

If you spot the grubs but your count is lower than six per square foot, baby your lawn to strengthen its natural defenses. Mow on higher blade settings and water thoroughly but infrequently to encourage the grass to grow new, deep roots. Do not cut off more than one-third of the grass height at each mowing, to avoid stressing the plant.

An ounce of prevention

Inspect your turf periodically by pulling on patches that look unhealthy, or have a professional inspect your lawn if you suspect a problem.

tip A grub problem is often indicated by increased mole, bird and raccoon activity. They dig up and feed on grubs at night. This may sound good, but moles kill your grass along with the grubs.

GRUBS

1 Pierce lawn with a shovel in a U-shape. Peel back the lawn (as though rolling up a rug) and count the white grubs in a 1-sq.-ft. area.

2 Treat your lawn with an insecticide if the count is six to 10 grubs in a square foot. Follow the manufacturer's directions carefully. Or consult with a yard service.

Problem: Fairy ring

Symptoms: Fairy rings are circles approximately 3 to 8 ft. wide that consist of a dark green and fast-growing area of grass surrounding an inner area of partially dead or thin grass. Some rings also produce mushrooms.

Cause: Fairy rings are caused by fungi that live in the soil. As the fungi feed on organic matter, they release nitrogen, causing the grass to turn dark green. As the colony grows, it disturbs the flow of needed water to the turf roots, creating thin or dead spots. Fairy rings often begin with the decomposition of organic matter, such as an old tree stump buried under the lawn.

Remedy: By bringing up the color in the rest of your lawn with a nitrogen fertilizer, you can mask much of the overgreening of the fairy ring (Photo 1). Hand-aerating the ring will break up the fungus and allow the flow of water and other nutrients to the grass roots (Photo 2).

Recovery time: Generally fairy rings can be masked with the application of fertilizer, with results in 10 to 14 days. The grass within the ring will thicken up with aeration in about two to three weeks.

An ounce of prevention

Aeration will help with fairy rings, but maintaining a healthy lawn with a balanced fertilization program is essential. Apply three doses:

1. Apply 1/2 lb. per 1,000 sq. ft. in late April or early May to give the overwintering grass roots a bit of a boost.
2. Add no more than 1/2 lb. per 1,000 sq. ft. at the end of June or in early July when temperatures are not at their peak. Stimulating growth during a heat wave will stress the plants.
3. Spread 1 lb. per 1,000 sq. ft. at the end of October. The best root growth takes place when the soil temps are between 58 and 65 degrees F. The roots store energy over the winter, making the entire lawn healthier the following spring.

DO NOT FERTILIZE THE RING ITSELF

1 Spread 1/2 lb. of nitrogen fertilizer per 1,000 sq. ft. to green up your lawn, but skip the fairy ring zone. This masks the lush green of the fairy ring by blending it into the rest of your yard.

CORE PLUGS

2 Break up the fungi with a hand aerator ($20 at a home center or garden store). Punch holes every 2 to 4 in. throughout the ring and 2 ft. beyond.

DECAYING WOOD

3 Go "treasure" hunting if you see no improvement in three weeks. Dig out rotting stumps, roots, construction debris or other organic materials under your lawn.

Problem: Shade

Symptoms: Shaded grass will look thin and patchy. Some types of grass actually produce wider blades as the plant attempts to catch more rays. But they also produce far fewer blades, lending a spindly appearance to the lawn. The truth is, if your lawn gets less than six to eight hours of sun daily, you are unlikely to sustain lush grass.

Cause: Trees, buildings and bushes.

Remedy: There are no good remedies. You can increase the sunlight as much as possible by trimming trees and shrubs. Also try starting areas in shade with sod instead of seed. The sod will adjust to the lower level of light. Although all seed varieties have their shade limitations, try overseeding your thin area with a shady grass mix.

Or throw in the towel, grab your trowel and plant a shade-tolerant ground cover. Many will thrive where your turf withered. Lamium (dead nettle) and ajuga (bugleweed) collaborate nicely in providing lovely blooms and an enthusiastic, but not invasive, carpet. This pair fares well, with a hearty tolerance spanning zones 3 to 8, and can be planted right up to your grass. They are fairly low growers and won't get more than a few nicks from a lawn mower.

Also, mulching between the ground cover plants will help retain moisture. This is especially wise if your new shade garden is on a slope; mulch will help prevent your fledging plants from washing out in a hard rain.

Recovery time: The plants and mulch will immediately boost the appearance of an area that was once thin grass. It'll take a couple of seasons for the ground cover to become established and blanket the area.

Using a garden hoe, work up the shady area to remove any struggling grass. Plant ground cover or a shade garden.

An ounce of prevention
Avoid the frustration of sun-starved grass by starting a shade garden or ground cover in any area that doesn't receive six to eight hours of good light per day.

Problem: Thatch

THATCH

Symptoms: If your grass feels soft and spongy when you walk on it, your lawn may have a thatch buildup. Thatch is a fibrous mat of dead stalks and roots that settles between the lawn's green leaves and the soil (photo right). When this mat becomes greater than 3/4 in. thick, it can cause your lawn to suffer from heat and drought. Affected lawns will rapidly wilt and turn blue-green, indicating they're hot and dry.

Cause: Cutting off too much at each mowing (letting the grass get too long) and cutting too low. Both will produce more dead grass tissue than microbes and earthworms can recycle. Thatch can develop in any soil but is most often associated with high clay content. Other causes are overfertilization and frequent, light watering, which encourage a shallow root system.

Remedy: Slice open a section of your lawn (Photo 1). If your grass shows 3/4 in. or more of thatch, it's time to rent an aerator (about $70 per day). An aerator is a heavy machine that opens the soil by pulling up finger-size soil cores. The lawn will absorb more oxygen and water, which will encourage healthy microbe growth and give worms wiggle room.

> **CAUTION:**
> Call your local utility provider to mark your underground utility lines before you aerate.

Aerate in the spring or fall when the grass is growing but the weather is not too hot to stress the plants (Photo 2). If the machine isn't pulling plugs, your lawn may be too dry. To avoid this problem, water thoroughly the day before you aerate. You can also rake in topsoil (Photo 3) to increase the healthy microorganisms that aid thatch's natural decomposition. Topsoil is available at any garden center.

An ounce of prevention

1. Mow often and cut no more than one-third of the grass height.
2. Water your lawn less often but for longer periods to prevent shallow root systems.
3. Reduce the amount of fertilizer you spread at any one time.
4. Reduce the use of pesticides. This will help keep the worm and microorganism populations healthy.
5. Aerate at least once every year if your lawn is prone to thatch.

Recovery time: You can expect the thatch layer to decrease by about 1/4 in. per year, about the same rate at which it forms.

1 Slice the turf grass with a shovel and pry it back. If the thatch depth measures more than 3/4 in., aerate at least 3 in. deep.

THATCH

CORE PLUGS

2 Make two or three passes with an aerator until you've made 3-in.-deep holes 2 in. apart throughout your yard.

3 Spread 1/4 in. of topsoil on the yard's most thatchy areas and then rake vigorously to fill the holes with loose soil.

Renting a lawn aerator

If your goal is to have one of the nicest lawns on the block, you can go a long way toward achieving it with annual aeration.

When a lawn lacks sufficient air (a "compacted" condition), it grows slowly and becomes vulnerable to disease, insects and heat damage. The soil will become impermeable and shed water instead of absorbing it.

Gas-powered aerators are available at most tool rental stores. They're slow-moving but powerful machines, so ask the clerk for handling directions. An aerator weighs about 200 lbs., so be prepared for some heavy lifting or ask your rental store for a ramp to get it into a truck bed or van.

Cool-season grasses should be aerated in the late summer or early fall. Spring is best for warm-season types. (If you're not sure what type you have, take a sample to an expert at a local garden center.)

Resist the temptation to remove the thatch with a rented power rake. Power raking is less effective than aerating because it typically removes less than 15 percent of thatch and may damage the healthy grass as well.

39 Seed a **bare spot** in your yard

Dead spots on a lawn may be caused by disease, repeated dog visits or snow mold. Simply adding extra fertilizer or randomly scattering seed on the bad spot isn't going to revive it. Start over by digging out the old sod and disposing of it; don't put diseased sod in your compost bin.

Holding a spade at a low angle, scrape out the dead grass (including roots) from a circular area 6 in. greater around than the bad spot. Next, use the spade to level out the soil and cut in a pattern of seed furrows (see photo). This crosshatching will create the proper pattern and depth for new seed to germinate.

Select seed that matches the variety already planted in the lawn. You don't want the new growth to contrast starkly with your established lawn. Distribute a handful of the new seed over the prepared spot and "close the soil" using the back of a short-tined rake. Water the area lightly and frequently until the roots are established.

1/2" DEEP FURROWS, 1/2" APART IN A CROSSHATCH PATTERN

Prepare a small area for new seed by chopping 1/2-in.-deep slits in the soil with a spade. Make a crosshatch pattern by cutting parallel lines 1/2 in. between slits first in one direction, and then perpendicular to it.

Fix a **storm door closer**

A heavy wind can catch a storm door and whip it open like a sail, tearing out the closer mounting bracket and cracking the door frame. And often the mounting screws strip and loosen from heavy wear.

Fixing the problem used to involve the tricky job of patching the old holes or even splicing in new trim. However, a product called the "Ultra Jamb Reinforcer" ($8 plus $6 shipping) eliminates all that hassle. It's available by calling (412) 370-0888 or visiting www.ultrajamb.com. This product includes a new closer bracket, mounting hardware and a heavy-duty steel plate that reinforces the door frame. The steel plate can be mounted anywhere on the door frame, accommodating virtually any type of closer bracket.

To begin, remove the old bracket as shown in Photo 1. Pop the

pin to release the piston arm and discard the old bracket. To install the reinforcer, mark and drill the eight mounting holes for the steel plate (Photos 2 and 3). Make sure to mount the plate parallel to the frame edges. This plate will allow you to drill new mounting holes in sound wood, and should cover most trim damage caused by the old bracket. Fill and paint any cracks not covered by the steel plate. Mount the steel plate to the door frame with the eight No. 6 wood screws enclosed in the package.

The new closer bracket is mounted to the steel plate with four No. 10 machine screws (Photo 4). Be sure to position the closer bracket so the angled edge faces the storm door. This provides the required spacing between the doorjamb and storm door, allowing the closer to function properly. Connect the piston arm to the new bracket with the piston pin and test the door.

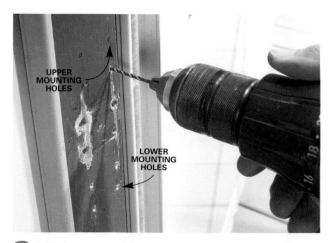

1 Lock the storm door all the way open. Remove the old closer bracket screws and bracket. Pull out the piston pin and discard the old bracket.

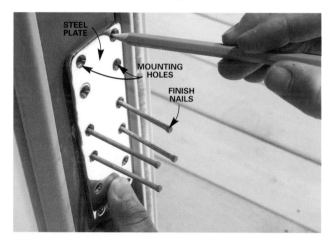

2 Slide small finish nails through the new steel plate and into the old screw holes to align it. Mark the eight mounting holes.

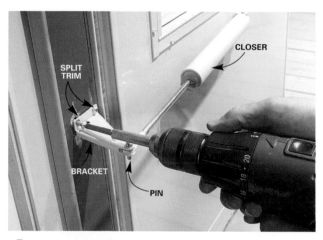

3 Drill the upper and lower mounting holes with a 3/32-in. drill bit.

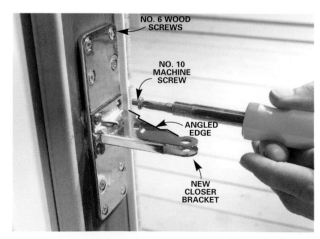

4 Screw the steel plate to the door frame with wood screws. Mount the closer bracket to the steel plate with machine screws. Make sure the angled edge of the bracket faces the storm door.

41 Fix a **door that doesn't latch**

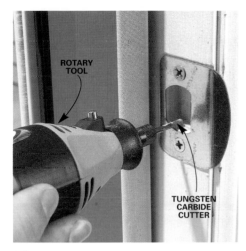

1 Shave off the inside of the strike plate with a rotary tool and a metal-cutting carbide bit. Remove a small amount and test the latch by closing the door. Continue removing metal until the door latch catches.

As a house settles, doorknob latches and strike plates sometimes become misaligned, so doors won't latch shut. Usually you have to push the door in, and either pull up or press down on the doorknob in order to get the latch to catch in the strike plate.

If the movement has been slight, there's a very simple fix for the problem. Instead of moving the strike plate, slightly enlarge the latch opening in the strike plate as shown here. A rotary tool does this quickly and easily. Use a carbide-cutting bit specifically designed for metal cutting.

Judge the part of the strike plate that needs grinding by testing when the latch catches. If you have to push down on the doorknob, then the top of the strike plate hole needs grinding. If the door has to be pushed in, then grind the outside edge of the strike plate hole.

You don't want the latch slopping around inside a huge opening, so don't grind away half the strike plate. Remove small amounts of metal and then test the door. Repeat until the door latch effortlessly catches the strike plate.

> **CAUTION:**
> Grinding metal can throw sparks and fragments into the air, so wear safety glasses with side shields, or full goggles when grinding. Otherwise, use a small round file.

42 Fix **loose hinges**

One day the door closes smoothly; the next day it's sticking. And the sticking grows worse as the weeks pass. It's a common old-house problem, but it can happen anywhere kids hang from doorknobs.

The screws holding the top hinges carry most of the weight of the door and are almost always the first to pull out, especially after they've been repeatedly tightened over the years (inset photo). The best way to beef them up is to replace the standard 3/4-in. hinge screws with at least two 3-in. screws that go through the jambs and solidly anchor into the framing. If the door has a large hinge with four screw holes, just drive 3-in. screws straight through the two holes toward the center of the door. However, if the hinge has only three holes, add a 3-in. screw through the middle hole and redrill the top screw hole at a slight angle so the screw hits solid wood (photo right).

Start the drill bit at a sharp angle so the bit doesn't follow the old screw hole. As soon as you feel a fresh hole starting, tip the drill bit back to an angle that will hit the stud—the angle shown here should work for most doors. If the bit or screw seems to be sliding off to the side between the drywall and the wood, redrill at a sharper angle.

Screw the hinge back in with yellow dichromate (zinc-plated) screws—the color and head size of these rust-resistant drywall screws are a good match for standard brass hinge screws. If the door doesn't shut properly after all the screws are driven in, they may have been driven in too far, pulling the door frame out of plumb. Just back the screws out a few turns.

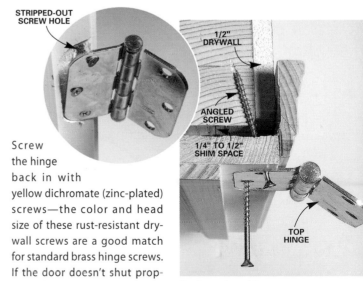

Replace short hinge screws with long screws when the screw holes no longer hold. Angle the long screws toward the studs to make sure they catch.

43 Unstick a sliding door

Years of dirt, exposure to the elements and hard use can turn sliding doors into sticking doors, but the problem is usually easy to fix.

Start with a good cleaning. Scrub caked dirt and grime out of the track with a stiff brush and soapy water. If the door still doesn't slide smoothly, the rollers under the door either need adjusting or are shot.

Locate the two adjusting screws at the bottom of the door (on the face or edge of the door) and pry off the trim caps that cover the screws. If one side looks lower, raise it until the door looks even on the track (Photo 1). If the door still sticks, turn both screws a quarter turn to raise the whole door. Then slide the door just short of the jamb and be sure the gap is even.

If the door still doesn't glide smoothly, you'll have to remove the door and examine the rollers. Unscrew the stop molding on the inside of the jamb (Photo 2). Be sure to hold the door in place once the stop is removed—if you forget and walk away for a moment, the door will fall in, requiring a much bigger repair! Tilt the door back (Photo 3) and set it on sawhorses. Inspect the rollers for problems. If they're full of dirt and debris, give them a good cleaning and a few drops of lubricant (like WD-40) and see if they spin freely. However, if the rollers are worn, cracked or bent, remove them (Photo 4) and replace them with a new pair ($8 to $16 a pair).

You can order rollers and other door parts through lumberyards and home centers or online (www.alcosupply.com or www.blainewindow.com). Look for the door manufacturer's name on the edge of the door or the hardware manufacturer's name on the roller.

ROLLERS

1 Lift or lower the door on the track with a screwdriver or Allen wrench. Raise it just enough to clear the track and roll smoothly.

HIDDEN ADJUSTING SCREW

TRIM CAP

2 Remove the screws that hold the stop molding. Cut the paint or varnish line on the room side of the stop molding so the molding will pull off cleanly.

STOP MOLDING

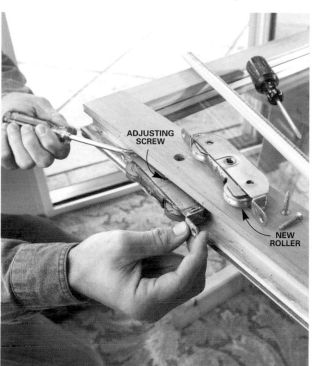

3 Grip the door by the edges and tip it about a foot into the room. Lift it up and out of the track one edge at a time.

4 Unscrew and pry out the screws that hold the roller in, then carefully lever it out with a screwdriver. Clean or replace the rollers.

ADJUSTING SCREW

NEW ROLLER

44 Free a sticking storm door

If your storm door won't close without a firm tug—or it won't close at all—it's probably rubbing against the frame, wearing off the paint and grating on your nerves. Most storm doors are mounted on a metal frame that's screwed to wood molding surrounding the door. When the metal frame on the hinge side of the door comes loose, or the molding itself loosens, the door sags and scrapes against the other side of the frame, usually near the top.

Before you grab your tools, partly open the door from the outside and push the door up and down. Watch the hinge side of the door frame. If the molding moves, secure it with extra nails (Photo 1). Start by adding a couple of nails near the top of the wood trim. Then add nails farther down if necessary. Sink the nailheads slightly with a nail set, cover the heads with acrylic caulk and touch up the molding with paint.

More often than not, it's the metal frame that comes loose, not the wood trim. To fix the metal frame, buy a few No. 8 x 1-in. pan head screws. Stainless steel screws are best. Stick a shim between the door and the frame (as in Photo 1), tighten the existing screws and drill new screw holes through the frame. Press lightly as you drill the metal; you don't want to drill into the wood molding with the 3/16-in. bit. Then drill a 3/32-in. pilot hole into the wood and add screws (Photo 2). In most cases, two or three screws added near the top of the frame will do the job.

SHIM KNOB SIDE

1 Position the door by wedging a shim between the door and the frame. Predrill and drive 10d galvanized finish nails to firmly fasten the molding.

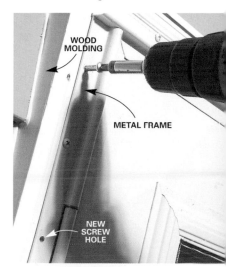

WOOD MOLDING

METAL FRAME

NEW SCREW HOLE

2 Drill new 3/16-in. screw holes through the metal frame. Then drill 3/32-in. pilot holes into the wood and drive in No. 8 x 1-in. screws. For a neater look, spray-paint the screw heads first.

45 Repair a damaged screen

Balls hit them, kids push on them and pets try to run through them. Whether your screens are aluminum or fiberglass, they'll get punctured or torn. Repairing a damaged screen is easy and takes only a few minutes.

If the screen's aluminum frame is in good shape, you'll need only the following: a roll of new screen material, a package of spline (the thin rubber strip that holds the screen material on the frame) and a screen rolling tool. You'll find all these items at home centers and hardware stores.

The steps shown here apply only to aluminum frame screens.

Selecting screen material

The most popular replacement screen material is fiberglass, as shown here. Its flexibility makes it the easiest to use—if you make a mistake, you can take it out of the frame and try again. Aluminum screen is sturdier, but you only get one chance. The grooves you've made with the screen rolling tool are there to stay.

A third type of screen material that's popular is sun-shading fabric. It blocks more sun, which means less load on your air-conditioning system and less fading of your carpet, draperies and furniture. It's also stronger than fiberglass and aluminum screening, so it's great for pet owners.

tip — If your long screens don't have a support, you can make one out of aluminum frame stock. It's located near the screening supplies in most stores. The aluminum stock can be cut with tin snips and trimmed to fit.

All three materials come in gray or black to match your other window screens. You can also get shiny aluminum as well as sun-shading fabrics in bronze and brown tones. Know the size of your window when you go to the home center. It will sell premeasured rolls to fit

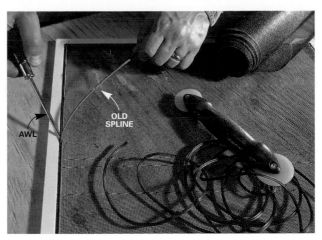

1 Pry out the old spline with an awl or a narrow-tipped screwdriver. Throw it away—spline gets hard and brittle as it ages and shouldn't be reused.

nearly any opening. If your screen frame is taller than 36 in., it should have a center support to keep it from bowing in once the material is in place. Newer screens usually come with this support.

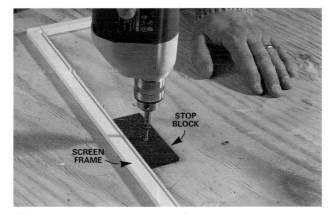

2 Place wooden blocks along the inside of the two longest sides of the frame and secure them to the work surface. The blocks keep the frame from bowing inward when you install the new screen material.

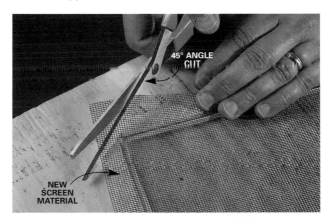

3 Lay the new screen material over the frame. It should overlap the frame by about 3/4 to 1 in. Cut each corner at a 45-degree angle just slightly beyond the spline groove. The cuts keep the screen from bunching in the corners.

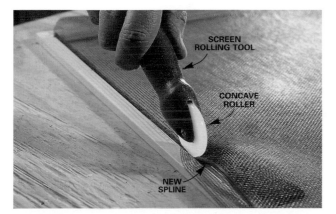

4 Begin installing the new spline at a corner. Use the screen rolling tool to push the spline and screen material into the groove. Continue around the frame. If wrinkles or bulges appear, remove the spline and reroll. Small wrinkles should tighten up as you get back to the starting corner.

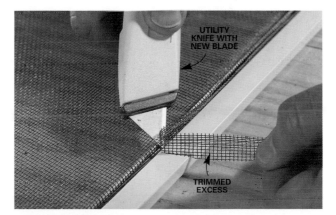

5 Trim excess screen material using a utility knife with a new sharp blade. A dull blade will pull the material, not cut it. Cut with the blade on top of the spline and pointed toward the outside of the frame.

46 Take out dents in a steel door

Fill a dent or hole in a steel door the same way a body shop would fix your car. You can do this with the door in place, but it will be easier with the door lying flat on sawhorses. Remove an area of paint a couple of inches larger than the damaged spot (Photo 1). Sand away the paint with 60- or 80-grit paper, or do the job faster with a small wire wheel ($7) in a drill. Next, fill the dent with auto body filler ($10 at hardware stores and home centers). To mix the filler, place a scoop of resin on a scrap of plywood or hardboard. Then add the hardener. Mix the two components thoroughly; unmixed resin won't harden and you'll be left with a sticky mess. A plastic putty knife ($1) makes a good mixing tool.

Apply the filler with a metal putty knife that's wider than the damaged spot (Photo 2). The filler will start to harden in just a couple of minutes, so you have to work fast. Fill the repair flush with the surrounding surface. Don't overfill it and don't try to smooth out imperfections after the filler begins to harden. Adding another coat of filler is easier than sanding off humps. When the filler has hardened completely (about 30 minutes), sand it smooth (Photo 3). After priming the repair, you can paint over the primer only. But the new paint won't perfectly match the older paint, so it's best to repaint the entire door.

1 Remove paint around the dent with a wire wheel. Roughen the bare metal with 60- or 80-grit sandpaper.

2 Mix auto body filler and fill the dent using a wide putty knife. Avoid leaving humps or ridges. If necessary, add more filler after the first layer hardens.

3 Sand the filler smooth with 100-grit paper. Use a sanding block to ensure a flat surface. Prime the repair and paint the entire door.

 tip If the damage is near the bottom of the door, you can skip the repair and cover it with a metal kick plate ($25 at home centers and hardware stores). Kick plates are about 8 in. wide and come in lengths to match standard doors.

47 Fix your own furnace

A furnace can be intimidating—especially when it's not working. However, there is good news. Roughly a quarter of all service calls can be avoided with easy fixes that cost little or nothing.

Here you'll learn about the common culprits and what to do about them.

> **C A U T I O N :**
> Always turn off the shutoff switch (see No. 2 on p. 69) and turn the thermostat off or all the way down before changing the filter or working on the thermostat or furnace.

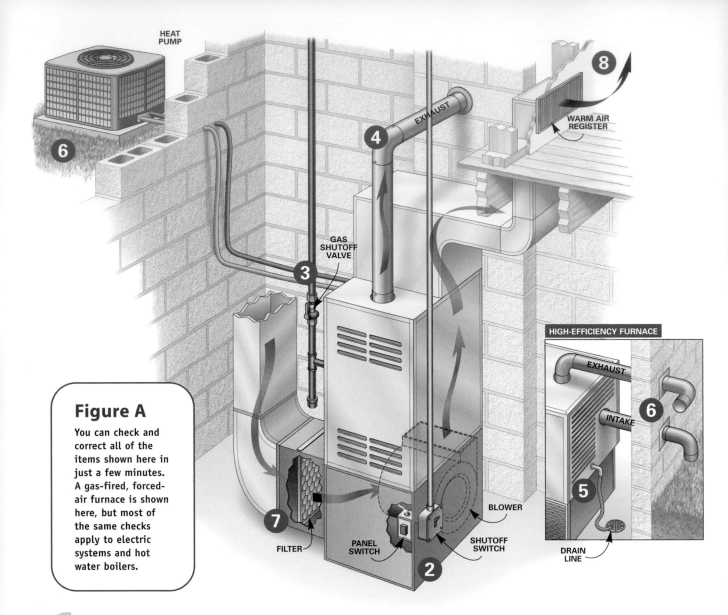

HEAT PUMP ⑥

GAS SHUTOFF VALVE ③

EXHAUST ④

⑧ WARM AIR REGISTER

HIGH-EFFICIENCY FURNACE

EXHAUST

INTAKE ⑥

⑤

DRAIN LINE

BLOWER

SHUTOFF SWITCH

PANEL SWITCH

FILTER ⑦

②

Figure A

You can check and correct all of the items shown here in just a few minutes. A gas-fired, forced-air furnace is shown here, but most of the same checks apply to electric systems and hot water boilers.

1 Check the thermostat to make sure it's on

Before you assume you have a furnace problem, check the thermostat to make sure it's actually telling the furnace to come on. Thermostats, especially programmable ones, can be complicated, and the more options a thermostat has, the more that can go wrong.

- Make sure the switch is on "Heat" rather than on "Cool."
- Check the temperature setting.
- Compare the temperature setting to the room temperature. Set the temperature five degrees higher than the room temperature and see if the furnace kicks on.
- Make sure the program is displaying the right day and time, as well as a.m. and p.m. settings.
- Trace the thermostat wires back to the furnace to check for breaks, especially if you've done

tip Lost your owner's manual? Most major-brand manuals are on the Web—just go to the manufacturer's Web site.

any remodeling recently. If you find a break in one of the thin wires, splice the line back together and wrap it with electrical tape.

- Replace the battery. If you have a power outage with a dead battery, you'll lose your settings and the thermostat will revert to the default program.
- Open the thermostat and gently blow out any dust or debris. Make sure the thermostat is level and firmly attached on the wall, and that none of the wires coming into it are loose.
- If you can't make the program settings work, you can bypass them altogether. Simply punch in the temperature you want with the up/down control and then press the hold button. That will switch on the furnace if the thermostat programming is the problem.

THERMOSTAT

HEAT OFF COOL FAN AUTO ON

2 Check shutoff switches and breakers

It sounds unbelievable, but furnace technicians often find that the only "repair" a furnace needs is to be turned on. Look for a standard wall switch on or near the furnace—all furnaces, no matter what age or type, have one somewhere. Check the circuit breaker or fuse for the furnace as well. Make sure the front panel covering the blower motor is securely fastened—there's a push-in switch under it that must be fully depressed for the furnace to operate.

3 Make sure the gas is on

Just as with switches, someone may have turned off a gas valve and then forgotten to turn it back on. Trace the gas line back from the furnace to the meter, and if you see a handle that's perpendicular to the gas pipe, turn it so it's parallel.

If you have an old furnace or boiler, you may have a pilot light. Remove the front panel and the burner cover and check to make sure it's lit.

4 Make sure the chimney exhaust flue is clear

Drawn by the warmth, birds sometimes fall into the chimney exhaust flue. Turn the furnace off and the thermostat all the way down, then dismantle the duct where it exits the furnace and check for debris. Be sure to reassemble the sections in the same order and direction that you took them out.

5 Flush out drain lines

High-efficiency furnaces can drain off several gallons of water a day in heating season. If the drain lines become restricted by sediment or mold growth, the furnace will shut down. If the drain hose looks dirty, remove the hose, fill it with a mixture of bleach and water (25 percent bleach), then flush it after several minutes.

6 Clean away leaves and debris from heat pumps or intake and exhaust vents

If you have a furnace that vents out the side of the house, make sure nothing is blocking the intake or exhaust. If either of the pipes is covered with screen mesh (like window screen), replace it with 1/2-in.-mesh hardware cloth. If ice is clogging one of the pipes, you have a bigger problem somewhere in the system.

7 Change filters

Dirty filters are the most common cause of furnace problems. Dust and dirt restrict airflow—and if the filter gets too clogged, the heat exchanger will overheat and shut off too quickly, and your house won't warm up. If the blower is running but no heat is coming out, replace the filter. A dirty filter also causes soot buildup on the heat exchanger, reducing the efficiency of the furnace and shortening its life.

The owner's manual shows where the filter is and how to remove it. Change inexpensive flat filters at least once a month. Make sure that the arrow points toward the furnace. Inspect pleated filters once a month. Hold them up to the light and if you can't see the light clearly through them, replace them. Manufacturers say pleated filters are good for three months, but change them more frequently if you have pets, kids or generate lots of dust.

8 Look for blocked or leaky ducts that restrict airflow

If your furnace comes on but one or two rooms are cold, first make sure all the room registers are open. Then examine any ductwork you can get access to and look for gaps between sections or branching points. Seal any gaps between sections of duct with special metal duct tape. Don't use standard cloth duct tape—it quickly deteriorates, and it may also cause ducts to leak if it was used to seal sections in the past.

Also check for handles protruding from the ductwork. These are dampers or air conditioner bypasses—make sure they're open.

Clear it off and call a technician to find out why it's happening.

If you have a heat pump, clear away grass and leaves from the fins of the outdoor compressor unit. Before heating season starts, hose it down gently from the top to rinse dirt and debris out of the housing.

Repair a **drywall crack**

As homes settle, cracks may radiate from the corners of doors and windows. Whether your walls are made of plaster or drywall, you can repair the cracks in two steps over a day or two—and get the area ready to sand and paint. Use paper tape; it's stronger than fiberglass tape for wall repairs. For cracks more than 1/4 in. deep, clean out the loose material and use a quick-setting crack filler like Durabond to build up the area level with the wall. Then use the steps shown in Photos 2 and 3 to fix it.

1 Cut a V-notch through the full length of the crack, 1/8 to 1/4 in. deep, removing all loose wall material. Protect woodwork with masking tape.

2 Embed paper tape in joint compound using a 6-in. taping blade. To avoid trapping air bubbles under the tape, moisten the paper tape with water, lay it over the crack and squeeze excess compound and air from underneath with the blade. Apply an additional thin layer of compound and feather it off 2 in. on both sides of the tape. Let dry.

3 Apply a second (and third, if necessary) coat of compound, smoothing it out 6 to 7 in. on both sides of the joint. Smooth the compound to a thin, even coat using long, continuous strokes with a 12-in. taping blade. Allow the repair to dry thoroughly, sand it smooth (avoid exposing the tape) and paint it.

Fix a **bouncy floor**

Assuming you have access to the underside of your floor joists, you can install either bridging or a layer of plywood to reduce the bounce in your floor. Try bridging first. Simply nail short I-joist sections between your existing joists (Photo 1). To prevent squeaks, apply construction adhesive to the top side of the bridging where it contacts your floor. If the joist span is shorter than 14 ft., install one row of bridging at the midpoint. If the span is longer than 14 ft., install two rows of bridging, one at one-third of the span and the other at two-thirds of the span.

If the floor is still too bouncy, glue and screw 1/2-in. plywood to the bottom of the joists (Photo 2). Start the first row at a corner, then stagger subsequent rows so the seams don't fall on the same joists. The drawback to this method is that you have to leave ceiling access to plumbing and gas valves, electrical boxes and other fixtures.

1 Toenail a line of I-joist blocks between the joists across the full length of the room.

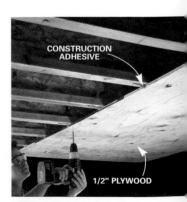

2 Fasten 4 x 8-ft. sheets of 1/2-in. plywood to the underside of the I-joists with 1-1/2-in. screws.

50 Replace a sink sprayer and hose

Over time, sink sprayers often break or become clogged with mineral deposits. Or the sprayer hose can harden and crack or wear through from rubbing against something under the sink. The best solution in these cases is replacement.

You can pick up just the sprayer head ($5) or a head and hose kit ($10) at a home center or hardware store.

Photo 1 shows how to remove the entire sprayer head and hose assembly. You may be able to get a small open-end wrench up to the sprayer hose nipple, but space is very tight. If there isn't enough room to turn the wrench, you'll have to purchase a basin wrench ($15 to $25 at home centers and hardware stores). If your sprayer hose is in good condition, simply unscrew the head and replace it (Photo 2).

1 Use an open-end or basin wrench to unscrew the sprayer hose from the hose nipple. Pull the old sprayer and hose out of the sink grommet. Slide the new hose through the grommet on top of the sink and reconnect it to the faucet.

2 Hold the base of the sprayer in your hand and twist off the sprayer head. Screw on the new head.

---

51 Relocate a sprinkler head

Decide where you want to relocate the sprinkler head. You can move it up to 4 ft. with flex pipe (available at plumbing and irrigation supply stores) without affecting performance. Dig an 8- to 12-in.-deep trench from the current head location to the new location. Turn off the irrigation system at the controller. Unscrew the sprinkler head from the riser (Photo 1) and then unscrew the riser. Insert a flex pipe elbow into the existing combination elbow or riser tee. Tighten the elbow until it's hand-tight. Then attach a 3/8-in. flex pipe to the flex pipe elbow by sliding it over the nipple (the flex pipe has a smaller diameter than the water line pipe). The connection doesn't require clamps.

Fasten a flex pipe elbow to the other end of the pipe. Place the sprinkler head on the elbow, then turn it until it's hand-tight. Hold the sprinkler head in the location you want it. The top of the head should be at ground level. Backfill around the head with your free hand (Photo 2). Once the head is secure, fill in the trench and replace the sod.

Note: Before you do any digging, call the North American One-Call Referral System at (888) 258-0808 to have someone mark underground gas, electrical, water and telephone lines.

52 Replace damaged vinyl siding

Vinyl siding is tough, but not indestructible. If a falling branch or a well-hit baseball has cracked a piece of your siding, you can make it as good as new in about 15 minutes with a $5 zip tool (available at any home center) and a replacement piece of siding. It's as simple as unzipping the damaged piece and snapping in a new one.

Starting at one end of the damaged piece, push the end of the zip tool up under the siding until you feel it hook the bottom lip (Photo 1). Pull the zip tool downward and out to unhook the bottom lip, then slide it along the edge, pulling the siding out as you go. Then unzip any pieces above the damaged piece. Hold them out of the way with your elbow while you pry out the nails that hold the damaged piece in place (Photo 2).

Slide the replacement piece up into place, pushing up until the lower lip locks into the piece below it. Drive 1-1/4-in. roofing nails through the nailing flange. Space them about every 16 in. (near the old nail holes). Nail in the center of the nailing slot and leave about 1/32 in. of space between the nail head and the siding so the vinyl can move freely. Don't nail the heads tightly or the siding will buckle when it warms up.

With the new piece nailed, use the zip tool to lock the upper piece down over it. Start at one end and pull the lip down, twisting the tool slightly to force the leading edge down (Photo 3). Slide the zip tool along, pushing in on the vinyl just behind the tool with your other hand so it snaps into place.

It's best to repair vinyl in warm weather. In temperatures

1 Slide the zip tool along the bottom edge to release the vinyl siding from the piece below it.

below freezing it becomes less flexible and may crack.

The downside of replacing older vinyl siding is that it can be hard to match the style and color, and siding rarely has any identifying marks. The best way to get a replacement piece is to take the broken piece to vinyl siding distributors in your area and find the closest match. If the old vinyl has faded or you can't find the right color, take the broken piece to a paint store and have the color matched. Paint the replacement piece with one coat of top-quality acrylic primer followed by acrylic house paint—acrylic paint will flex with the movement of the vinyl.

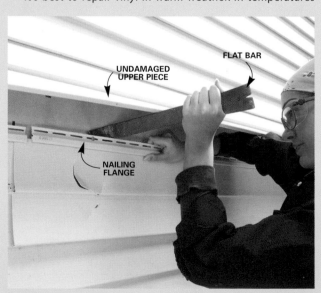

2 Slip a flat bar behind the damaged piece of vinyl siding and pry out the nails.

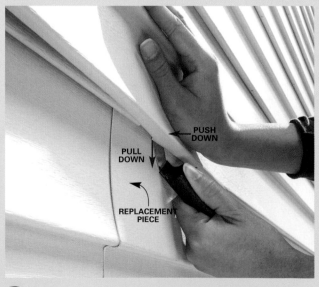

3 Install the replacement piece and hook the lip of the upper siding piece into the slot to lock it into place.

53 Unclog a faucet

If the flow from your kitchen or bathroom faucet isn't what it used to be, the aerator is probably plugged. An aerator can clog slowly as mineral deposits build up, or quickly after plumbing work loosens debris inside pipes. Usually, a quick cleaning solves the problem. Remove the aerator (Photo 1) and disassemble it. You may need a small screwdriver or knife to pry the components apart. Scrub away any tough buildup with an old toothbrush (Photo 2) and rinse each part thoroughly (be sure to close the drain stopper). Gunk can also build up inside the faucet neck, so ream it out with your finger and flush out the loosened debris.

If the mineral buildup resists scrubbing and you have a standard cylinder-shaped aerator, you can replace it (about $5). Take your old aerator along to the home center or hardware store to find a match. If your aerator has a fancy shape (like the one shown here), finding a match won't be as simple. So try this first: Soak the aerator parts in vinegar overnight to soften mineral buildup. If that doesn't work, go to any online search engine and type in the brand of your faucet followed by "faucet parts." With a little searching, you can find diagrams of your faucet and order a new aerator. Expect to spend $10 or more for a nonstandard aerator.

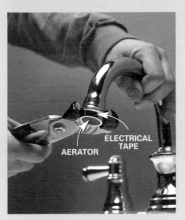

1 Wrap the pliers' jaws and the aerator with electrical tape and unscrew the aerator. Close the stopper so the small parts can't fall down the drain.

2 Disassemble the aerator and lay out the parts in the order you remove them to make reassembly foolproof. Scrub the parts and reassemble them.

54 Remove tough stains from vinyl flooring

Sheet vinyl "resilient" flooring is so easy to clean that it may never require anything beyond damp mopping with a cleaner intended for vinyl floors. But if your floor has marks or stains that still won't come off, you can use stronger stuff. Although the methods described here won't harm most vinyl floors, test them first in a closet or on a section of flooring that's hidden by furniture. Use white rags only; chemicals that dissolve stains can also make fabric colors bleed and stain your floor.

Isopropyl alcohol, sold as a disinfectant at drug stores ($4), is a mild solvent. It's the best cleaner for heel marks and works on other tough stains too. You can also use lighter fluid or mineral spirits. Remember that all these products are flammable; turn off any nearby pilot lights and hang rags out to dry before throwing them away.

Bleach will often erase stains left by liquids like fruit juices, tomato sauce and wine. Mix one part household bleach with four parts water, soak a rag in it and lay the rag over the stain. Bleach works slowly; you may have to leave the rag in place for an hour or so.

Oxalic acid is the solution for stubborn rust stains. It's often labeled "wood bleach"—but not all wood bleach contains oxalic acid, so check the label. Most paint stores and some hardware stores carry oxalic acid ($7). If the stain won't rub off, wet a rag with the acid solution and lay it over the stain for 10 minutes. If the stain remains, rewet the rag and repeat. When that's done, rinse the floor with clean water.

1 Dampen a white rag with isopropyl alcohol and rub away heel marks.

2 Mix oxalic acid powder with water and dab rust stains to remove them. Protect your hands with rubber gloves and open a window for ventilation.

55 Turn threshold screws to seal out **drafts**

ADJUSTABLE THRESHOLD

Those big screwheads in the threshold of a newer entry door aren't just decorative; they raise or lower a narrow strip set in the threshold. So if you've noticed a draft under the door, try this: On a sunny day, turn off the lights and close nearby curtains. Lie down and look for daylight under the door. A sliver of light sneaking in at both corners of the door is normal. But if you see light between the threshold and the door, grab your screwdriver. Raise the threshold where light enters by turning the nearest screws counterclockwise. Set a straightedge (such as a framing square) on the threshold and adjust the other screws to make sure the adjustable strip is straight. Close the door and check for light. Readjust the threshold until you've eliminated the light. But don't raise the threshold so high that it presses too hard against the weatherstripping on the door. A too-tight fit will wear out the weatherstripping quickly.

56 Shim **gapping doors**

If you have big gaps along the latch side of your doors, they were probably prehung in their frames at the factory and installed as a unit. The installer should have adjusted the frame with shims to leave about a 1/8-in. gap along the latch side, about the thickness of two quarters (coins). Sometimes the gap is far too wide.

To readjust the door frame, you have to remove the trim along the latch side to get at the shims. This job can be a hassle, especially if you have painted trim. So try this trick first. Slip a 1/16-in.-thick cardboard strip behind each hinge (Photos 1 and 2). This will widen the gap along the hinge side and narrow the gap along the latch side. Hopefully, it'll be enough to make the latch solid.

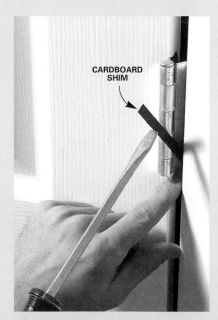

CARDBOARD SHIM

1 Loosen the hinge screws in the jamb and insert a 1/16-in.-thick x 3/8-in.-wide piece of cardboard behind the hinge leaf. Push it against the screws and retighten them.

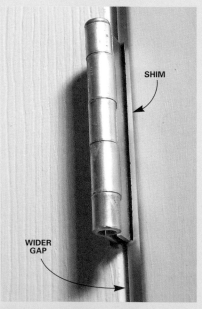

SHIM

WIDER GAP

2 Follow the same procedure for each hinge. The gap along the hinge side should open about 1/16 in. and narrow the gap on the latch side.

57 Tighten a floppy **faucet handle**

If you have a loose valve handle—on a shower, bathroom or kitchen faucet—tighten the screw that holds the handle in place. With some faucets, you'll have to pry off the metal button at the center of the handle. With others, you'll find a setscrew near the base of the handle. Setscrews usually require a hex (or "Allen") wrench. If tightening doesn't work, the stem inside the handle may be worn, especially if it's plastic. Here's a trick to tighten worn stems on most types of faucets: Wrap the stem tightly with Teflon pipe thread tape and slip the handle back over the stem. In most cases, a single wrap creates a snug fit.

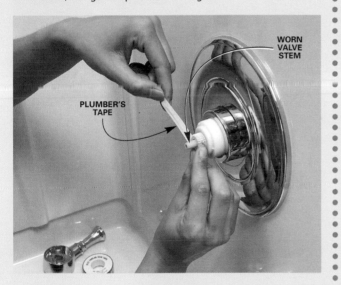

WORN VALVE STEM

PLUMBER'S TAPE

58 Fix bad **wallpaper** seams

Repairing loose seams is fairly simple and doesn't require a steamer. Just apply a seam repair adhesive. It provides a solid bond and will keep the seams from coming loose. It's available at paint stores and home centers for less than $10.

Squirt the adhesive directly onto the wall behind the loose seams, then press the edges back into place. Use a roller or straightedge as shown to firmly press the paper against the wall and drive out any air bubbles. Wipe away any excess adhesive with a damp sponge.

ROLLER

REPAIR ADHESIVE

59 Straighten bubbling **wallpaper**

Fix the bubbles by cutting them with a razor knife. A small slit is all that's needed. Then insert the end of a glue applicator in the slit and squeeze in a little adhesive (see photo).

Wipe away excessive adhesive with a damp sponge and press the wallpaper against the wall to force out the air, using a plastic straightedge.

The glue applicators and proper adhesive are available at paint stores and home centers for less than $10.

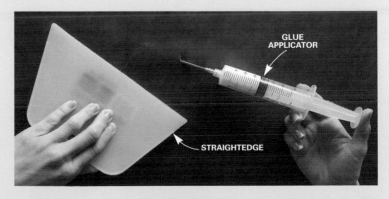

GLUE APPLICATOR

STRAIGHTEDGE

60 Push-button **disposer** fix

If your disposer won't start, push the reset button and give it a spin. All disposers have an overload feature that automatically shuts off the power when the motor becomes overloaded and gets too hot. Once the motor cools, simply push the reset button on the side of or under the unit (photo left).

On the other hand, if it hums but doesn't spin, it may have something stuck in it. Switch the disposer off, then try working through it by turning the blades with a special disposer wrench ($10 at home centers) or by turning a bottom bolt (photo right). Many disposers have an Allen wrench for that purpose, inset on the bottom of the machine.

61 Reset the **GFCI**

If the circuit breaker hasn't tripped and your appliance isn't working, look for a tripped GFCI. When a light goes out or a switch doesn't work, first check the main electrical panel for a tripped circuit breaker. But don't stop there. Before you change out lightbulbs and switches, see if a GFCI outlet (which may be upstream from the troubled light or outlet) has tripped. Sometimes all the bathrooms or the outside lights are powered through a single GFCI located in one bathroom or elsewhere, such as in a basement. Simply push the reset button on the GFCI and you could be back in business.

62 Clean the **dishwasher** filter

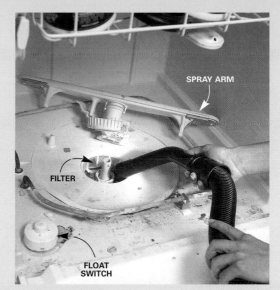

SPRAY ARM

FILTER

FLOAT SWITCH

When your dishwasher no longer gets your dishes clean, a food-filled filter is most often to blame. If it's clogged, water can't make it to the spray arms to clean the dishes in the top rack. The fix takes two minutes. Simply pull out the lower rack and remove the filter cover inside the dishwasher. (Check your owner's manual if you can't spot the filter.) Then use a wet vacuum to clean off the screen.

While you're there, slide the nearby float switch up and down. If it's jammed with food debris, you won't get any water. If the cover sticks, jiggle it up and down and clean it with water.

63 Quiet a noisy **washer**

When a washing machine cabinet rocks, it makes a horrible racket during the spin cycle. The solution is to simply readjust the legs. Screw the front legs up or down until the cabinet is level. When both legs are solid on the floor, tighten each leg's locking nut. In most washers, to adjust the rear legs, gently tilt the machine forward and gently lower it down. The movement will self-adjust the rear legs.

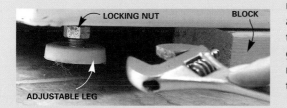

LOCKING NUT   **BLOCK**

ADJUSTABLE LEG

64 Change the **dryer filter**

If your clothes are damp after a normal cycle, check the dryer setting—make sure it's not on "fluff air," a non-heat setting.

Another common cause of poor drying is a clogged lint filter. The filter may look clean, but it may actually be covered by a nearly invisible film caused by dryer sheets. This film reduces airflow and forces the thermostat to shut off the heat before your clothes are dry. Pull out the filter and scrub it in hot water with a little laundry detergent and a stiff kitchen brush.

Also check the outside dryer vent for any lint that may have built up there. The louver door–style vent covers are notorious for lint buildup, which traps heat and turns the heat off in the dryer. Pull the cover completely off to get to these clogs.

FLUFF AIR

DRYER FILTER

65 Change the air conditioner thermostat

If you turn your central air conditioner on, off and then on again in rapid order, chances are you'll blow a fuse or shut off a circuit breaker or the air conditioner simply won't respond. That's because the compressor (in the outdoor condensing unit) may have stopped in a high compression mode, making it difficult to start until the compression releases. Older condensing units may switch the compressor on anyway, which causes the circuit to overload and blow a fuse. Newer, "smarter" condensing units will prevent this blunder by delaying the AC's "on" function for a few minutes. It's easy to mistake this delay for a faulty air conditioner. Be patient and give the air conditioner about five minutes to come back on.

To determine if you have a blown fuse, locate the special fuse block near the outside unit. Pull out the block and take the whole thing to the hardware store. A salesperson can test the cartridge fuses and tell you if you need to replace them.

Another simple reason your AC might not come on: You've signed up for a cost discount with your electric company in

CARTRIDGE FUSE

FUSE BLOCK

FUSE BLOCK

AIR CONDITIONER SHUTOFF BOX

CONDENSING UNIT (INCLUDES COMPRESSOR)

exchange for limited air conditioning during high-demand periods, and you're in an "off" period. If you can't remember, call your electric company to find out. You don't want to pay the repair technician to drive out and explain this program to you!

66 Lubricate sticking drawers

Candle wax is a handy lubricant for old drawers or any furniture that has wood sliding against wood. Just rub a candle hard against the skids under the drawer. Rub the tracks inside the chest or cabinet too.

67 Lubricate sticking locks

If your lock turns hard or your key doesn't slide in smoothly, the lock might be worn out. Then again, it may just need lubrication. Squirt a puff of powdered graphite into the keyhole. Unlike liquid lubricants, graphite won't create sticky grime inside the lock. A tube costs about $3 at home centers.

In this chapter you'll find quick, easy and inexpensive ways to improve the look and functionality of your home. Some projects improve curb appeal or make the interior more attractive, others help you get organized, while others save you money.

Chapter 3

home improvements

⑥⑧ Decorate with simple stenciling

Stenciling is a traditional decorative technique that perfectly complements a Craftsman-style room. And it's perfectly easy to learn, too. If you can handle a paintbrush and a tape measure, you can quickly master the techniques for applying an attractive, simple border. And with a little practice, you can tackle complex patterns using multiple stencils and colors—and even create your own designs.

The key tools are a special stenciling brush ($10; Photo 2) and the stencil and paint. A wide variety of each are available at craft and art supply stores. You can also find stencil patterns at bookstores or on the Internet, or even buy stencil blanks and cut your own with an X-Acto knife. The stencil shown here, a pattern called Ginkgo Frieze, is available from www.fairoak.com for $42. Match the brush size to the area being filled within the stencil. A 1/2-in., medium-size brush, shown here, is a good, all-purpose size. You can use almost any paint—artist acrylics, wall paints or the special stenciling paints sold at craft and art supply stores. Artist acrylic paint is shown here.

Plan the layout

Position your stencil on the wall at the desired height and mark the alignment holes or top edge. Then snap a light, horizontal chalk line around the room at that height. Make sure that whatever color chalk you use wipes off easily. Or use faint pencil marks, which can be easily removed or covered later.

The key to a good layout is to avoid awkward pattern breaks at doors, windows and corners. To work out the best spacing, measure the stencil pattern and mark the actual repetitions on the wall. Vary the spacing slightly as needed to make the pattern fall in a pleasing way. Or if your stencil has multiple figures, you can alter the spacing between them. Start your layout at the most prominent part of the room and make compromises in less visible areas. Draw vertical lines at the pattern center points to make positioning easier.

Dab on the paint

Tape the stencil pattern on the alignment marks (Photo 1) and put a small quantity of paint on a paper plate. Push the stenciling brush into the paint just enough to coat the tips of the bristles, then pat off the excess on a dry cloth or newspaper, making sure the paint spreads to all the bristles (Photo 2). The brush should be almost dry—remember, it's easier to add paint than it is to take it away.

Lightly dab on the paint (Photo 3). Hold the stencil pattern with your free hand to keep it still and flat. Don't worry about getting paint on the stencil, but avoid wiping or stabbing too

1 Snap lines on the wall to align with the alignment marks on your stencil. Tape the stencil in place along the top edge with removable masking tape.

2 Dab the special stenciling brush into the paint, then pat off the bristles on a dry cloth. Leave the brush almost dry.

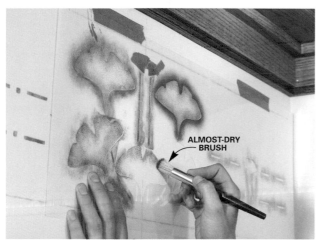

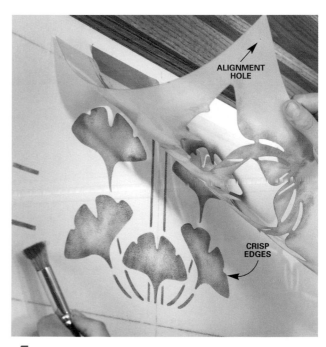

3 Apply the paint to the stencil with light dabbing and swirling motions until the stencil area is covered. Work in from the edges, brushing toward the center.

hard around the edges. You can cover the cutout completely or work for shading effects. Cover nearby cutouts with masking tape so you don't accidentally get paint in them (Photo 5).

Mistakes are easy to correct. You can lift the stencil (Photo 4) and wipe off any paint that's smeared under the edge with a damp paper towel, or touch it up later with wall paint. If you wipe some of the stenciled area away, just lay the stencil down again and touch up.

For two colors, mask off the cutout where the second color will go, stencil on the first color all the way around the room, then go back and add the second color, following your original alignment marks (Photo 5). Other colors and even additional stencil patterns can be added in this manner.

4 Lift the stencil up on the tape hinges and check for paint drips and for clear, sharp edges. Lay the stencil back down and touch up if necessary.

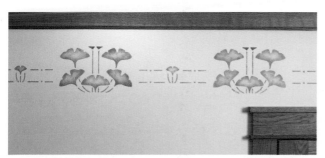

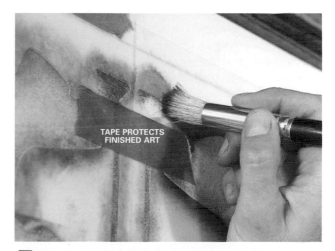

5 Allow the first color to dry, then tape the stencil up on the same marks and apply the second color. Cover nearby areas of the stencil to avoid getting paint in them.

69 Rejuvenate your cabinets

BEFORE

AFTER

Take a look, a really close look. At first glance it may be hard to recognize, but the kitchen in the inset is the same as the one above. The cabinet "boxes," the countertop, the layout, the flooring, the sink and the window haven't changed. The total cost for all of the cabinet upgrades shown here was $2,100 (not including the wall tile). With the average full-scale kitchen remodeling project costing more than $30,000 (and about one-third of that amount spent on cabinetry), you can see a big impact for a small cost.

If you're pleased with the basic layout and function of your kitchen but want to update the look—and add a few new features—read on. You'll learn how paint, new cabinet doors and drawer fronts, moldings and a few accessories can transform your kitchen.

Most of the projects require only a drill, basic hand tools and intermediate DIY savvy, although a power miter saw and pneumatic finish nailer allow you to cut and install the crown molding faster.

Bear in mind, these upgrades won't fix cabinets that are falling apart, create more storage space or make your kitchen easier to navigate. But if you want to give your kitchen an inexpensive yet dramatic face-lift, here's how.

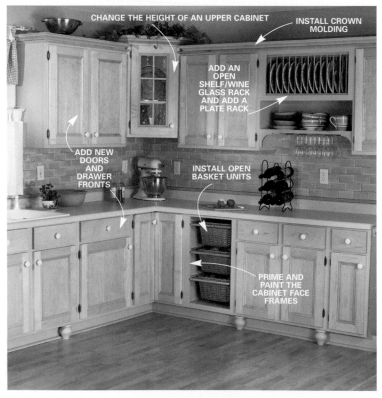

CHANGE THE HEIGHT OF AN UPPER CABINET

INSTALL CROWN MOLDING

ADD AN OPEN SHELF/WINE GLASS RACK AND ADD A PLATE RACK

ADD NEW DOORS AND DRAWER FRONTS

INSTALL OPEN BASKET UNITS

PRIME AND PAINT THE CABINET FACE FRAMES

Raise an upper cabinet

To break up the monotony of a row of cabinets, change the height of one or more upper cabinets. This provides more "headroom" for working and more space for lighting and appliances, as well as creates a more interesting and varied look.

In order to raise a cabinet, your cabinets must be the modular kind in which each cabinet is an independent "box" screwed to adjacent ones. "Builder cabinets," with the entire row of cabinets built and installed as one unit, aren't easily separated. If yours are modular, you can elevate the corner cabinet 3 in., temporarily prop it up with scrap lumber, drill pilot holes for new screws, then reattach it. A cabinet that's been in place a long time may need a sharp rap with a hammer to free it from paint and grime that have "glued" it in place.

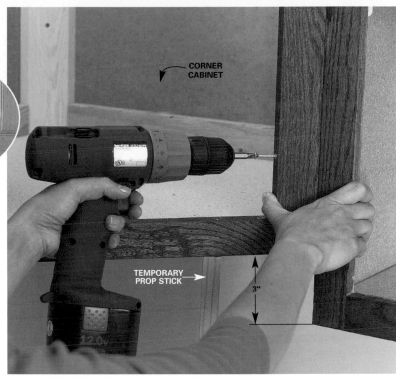

To raise a cabinet, remove the shelves and doors and then the screws securing it to the wall and cabinets on either side. Raise the cabinet, temporarily prop it in place, drill new pilot holes, then reinstall the screws.

Add an open shelf, wineglass rack and plate rack

If you have a short cabinet flanked by two taller cabinets, you can add this combination shelf/wine rack.

Cut the shelf to length, then add mounting strips on each end. Cut four 9-in. sections of wineglass molding from a 3-ft. length (see Buyer's Guide, p. 85), then glue and nail them to the bottom of the pine shelf. Cut curved brackets from each end of a 1x6 maple board and cut the center 1 in. wide to serve as shelf edging. Finally, install the unit by driving screws through the mounting strips and into the cabinets on each side.

To display your plates and keep them accessible and chip-free, build and install this plate rack. The total cost of materials is less than $10.

To create the two plate rack "ladders," measure the cabinet, then build each ladder so the finished height equals the height of the inside of the cabinet. The finished width should be equal to the width of the face frame opening. Drill 3/8-in. holes, 3/8 in. deep in 3/4-in. x 3/4-in.-square dowels and space them every 1-1/2 in. Cut the dowels to length, add a drop of glue in each hole, insert the dowels, then use elastic cords or clamps to hold things together until the glue dries.

A drill press comes in handy, but you can get excellent results using a cordless drill, a steady hand and a 3/8-in. drill bit with masking tape wrapped around it as a depth guide for the holes in the rails.

Build a shelf to fit snugly between the cabinets on each side. Use a jigsaw to create curved brackets, nail wine glass brackets to the bottom of the shelf, then install the entire unit as one piece.

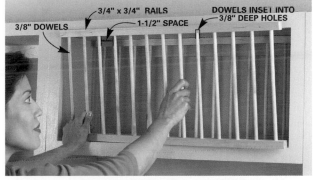

Cut, assemble and install the two plate rack "ladders." Use short screws to secure the ladders in the cabinet opening. Set the rear ladder 4 in. away from the back of the cabinet and the front ladder snug against the back of the face frame.

Add new doors and drawer fronts

A local cabinet shop can make new doors and drawer fronts the exact same dimensions as the old ones. Use the same hinges and mounting holes in the face frames to ensure the right fit. You can have your components made locally or by one of the companies listed in the Buyer's Guide, p. 85.

Existing drawer fronts can be attached in a number of different ways. You can probably pry off the old and screw on the new. If not, use a circular saw to cut all four edges of the drawer front even with the edges of the drawer box, then apply the new drawer front directly over the old. This will make your drawers 3/4 in. longer; make certain your drawer hardware and cabinets can accommodate the extra length. If not, you may need to install new drawer hardware or new drawer "boxes."

Mount the hinges to the doors, then mount the doors to the face frames using the existing screw holes. Most hinges allow for some up-and-down movement and tilt so the doors can be adjusted evenly.

Replace the old drawer fronts. Pry off the old front using a chisel and a flat bar, mark the position of the drawer box on the back of the new drawer front, then join the two using wood glue and screws.

Install crown molding

Crown molding comes in many profiles and sizes. Shown here is rope molding (see Buyer's Guide, p. 85). If your face frames aren't wide enough on top to nail the molding to, nail strips of wood to the top edge to provide a nailing surface.

Raising the corner cabinet may create a challenge where the moldings on each side butt into it. If that's the case with your cabinets, hold the upper part of the crown molding back a few inches, but extend the thin rope molding portion so it butts into the corner cabinet.

Position and mark each piece of crown molding as you work your way around the kitchen. Make small notches in the top corners of the face frames so the moldings lie flat against the sides of the cabinets when installed.

Cut the crown molding by placing it upside down and securing it at the correct angle with a clamp and wood scrap.

Paint cabinet face frames

Proper preparation and sanding between coats are the keys to a smooth, durable paint job on your cabinet face frames.

Oil paints arguably create the smoothest surface, since they dry slowly and "self-level" as brushstroke marks fill in. However, this slow drying time means they're more vulnerable to dust. Cleanup is also more of a hassle. Latex paints dry quickly and may show brushstrokes more, but additives like Floetrol (The Flood Co., 800-321-3444,

www.flood.com) improve "brushability." After priming, paint the cabinets with a gloss or semigloss paint. Apply a thin first coat, let it dry, then lightly sand with 120- or 180-grit sandpaper. Wipe the surface, then apply a second coat. Two or three thin coats are better than one or two thick ones.

If you have a gas stove, turn off the gas for safety while using mineral spirits, shellac or oil paints, and provide plenty of ventilation.

SANDING BLOCK WITH 120-GRIT PAPER

PIGMENTED SHELLAC PRIMER

Clean the cabinet face frames with mineral spirits, then scrub them with household ammonia and rinse. Fill holes with spackling compound, then sand with 120-grit sandpaper. Vacuum the cabinets, then prime them with a pigmented shellac. Lightly sand the dried primer.

Install open basket units

The "Base 18" baskets installed here (see Buyer's Guide, below) come with two side tracks that can be cut narrower to accommodate cabinets ranging in width from 15-7/8 in. to 17-7/8 in. "Base 15" baskets fit cabinets with an inside width of 12-7/8 in. to 15-7/8 in. Measure carefully, cut the basket tracks to width, then install them as shown.

FULL SAW

DRAWER OPENING

HORIZONTAL RAIL

DOOR OPENING

Remove cabinet hardware and the rails where you want to create an open cabinet. A fine-tooth pull saw works well for removing the dividers, since it lies flat against the cabinet frame as it cuts. Sand the area to create a smooth surface.

LEVEL LINE

BASKET TRACKS

Cut the tracks to the proper width, then level them in both directions and screw them to the sides of the cabinet.

Buyer's Guide

All the products used in these projects are readily available through catalogs, the Internet and specialty woodworking stores. Here are a few sources:

CABINET DOORS AND DRAWER FRONTS

There are a variety of mail order sources you can explore:

■ Custom Kitchen Cabinet and Refacing Co.: (888) 407-3322, www.reface.com

■ Jackson Custom Woodworks: www.jacksoncustom.com

■ Kitchen Door Depot: (877) 399-5677, www.kitchen-doordepot.com

■ Kitchen Doors Online: (877) 887-0400, www.kitchendoorsonline.net

■ Rockler Custom Door and Drawer Front Program: (800) 279-4441, www.rockler.com

CROWN MOLDING, BUN FEET, BASKETS, WINE GLASS MOLDING

You can order maple rope crown molding (No. 53639, $90 per 8-ft. length), wicker baskets (No. 47527, $65 to $69 each), wine glass molding (No. 22210, $13 per 36-in. piece) and bun feet (No. 70410, $10.60 each) from Rockler (800-279-4441, www.rockler.com).

Outwater (800-631-8375, www.outwater.com) and Woodworker's Supply (800-645-9292, www.woodworker.com) sell similar items.

MISCELLANEOUS

The porcelain pulls, dowels for the plate rack, primer and paint are available at home centers.

The wall tile is Newport, Sage Green by Walker Zanger Ceramics, (818) 252-4000, www.walkerzanger.com.

70 Boost your home's curb appeal

There are dozens of small, inexpensive improvements you can do that add up to a dramatic upgrade. Here you'll find a menu of ideas to consider.

Tackle first things first. If the paint on your house is peeling, faded or outdated, break out the paintbrush. No matter what other projects you do, your house will never reach maximum curb appeal with shabby-looking paint.

Also consider how much time you're willing to invest, in terms of both undertaking the project and maintaining it afterward. Lining a walkway with bricks or installing a screen door can eat up a day, but neither requires much maintenance. Installing a flower box is quick and easy but requires regular upkeep. And keep the big picture in mind. If you're replacing your old light fixture with a brass one, your door hardware and house numbers will probably look best in brass too.

Go at it, add your own touches and have fun!

Paint, paint, paint

Cost: $25 and up

Time: Half day and up

Whether you paint your front door, your trim or your entire house, few projects can transform a house as dramatically and inexpensively as paint. Top-notch paint costs only a few dollars more per gallon, but it will cover better, go on smoother and last longer than the cheap stuff—it's a smart investment.

A few rules of thumb: If you want a small house to look larger, paint it white. If your house is a mishmash of styles or has sagging soffits or other flaws, paint everything the same color to help visually unify the house.

Several paint manufacturers have computer software that allows you to mock up different paint color schemes on a digital image of your house (or on a house close in style supplied by the program). Visit www.glidden.com, www.benjaminmoore.com and www.sherwin-williams.com to find out more.

Install new house numbers

Cost: $1 and up for individual numbers; custom plaques start at about $50

Time: 1 hour

Replace shabby or dated-looking numbers with ones made of brass, aluminum or stainless steel. They'll look best if the finish matches that of any light fixtures and door hardware. You can buy do-it-yourself address plaque kits from Ace Hardware (www.acehardware.com). For custom plaques, contact www.addressplaques.net or www.bestnest.com.

Upgrade your mailbox

Cost: $10 and up

Time: 1 hour and up

Whether you have a box mounted to the house, a letter slot next to the door or a freestanding box on a post near the street, a new mailbox can add a splash of curb appeal. Purchase an approved mailbox and follow regulations regarding height; for example, curbside mailboxes must be mounted so bottoms are 42 to 48 in. above the ground. And remember, hanging plants and flowers growing around a mailbox may increase curb appeal, but the bees and other stinging insects these plants attract aren't always your mail carrier's best friend.

Visit www.mailboxworks.com for a wide selection of mailboxes and letter slots.

Line a walkway with bricks or pavers

Cost: $2 to $4 per linear foot
Time: Half to a full day

Is your concrete walkway in decent—but boring—shape? Adding color, texture and width to an existing walkway by lining it with pavers is a whole lot easier and cheaper than replacing it. Stone, clay and concrete pavers are all good choices. The basic procedure involves digging a trench one paver wide along the walkway, leveling in a bed of sand or pea gravel, then setting and tamping pavers so they're flush with the top of the walkway.

Replace a light fixture

Cost: $25 and up
Time: 1 to 2 hours

Consider function as well as style when selecting a fixture; it should light up your steps, house numbers and door without being too dominant. To simplify the project, buy a fixture that has the same mounting system or screw spacing as the existing fixture.

Make certain the power is off and the new fixture is rated for exterior use before installing it. Some sconce-style lights are now available with unobtrusive, built-in motion detectors.

Plant a tree

Cost: $30 and up
Time: 2 to 4 hours

Plant a tree and you get not only curb appeal but also shade, an improved view from the inside, and with some trees, fall color. Before planting, determine the mature size of the tree. Plant it far enough away from the house so limbs won't overhang the roof or cause other problems. A tree planted in the right place can help block wind and act as a mini solar device by screening out the hot summer sun when it's in full leaf and letting in welcome winter sunshine when it's leafless. Consider planting two trees to "frame" the house or entryway. Foundation plantings are another way to add appeal.

Add low-voltage lighting

Cost: $50 and up
Time: 2 hours and up

Low-voltage lighting can dramatically improve your home's nighttime curb appeal, and by lighting walkways and dark corners, it can improve safety and security as well. Lighting can be grouped into three basic categories: downlights, uplights and specialty lights. Buy a transformer that includes a timer or light sensor so the lights automatically turn on and off.

Install shutters

Cost: About $4 per sq. ft. for standard vinyl shutters; $25 to $50 per sq. ft. for custom-made wood shutters
Time: 1 to 2 hours to paint, 1/2 to 1 hour to install

Decorative shutters can add color, quaintness and depth to a house. Shutters with louvers or raised panels have a traditional look; those with decorative cutouts have more of a cottage or country feel.

For an authentic look, mount wood shutters using special shutter hinges and keep them pinned against the house with old-fashioned shutter dogs. Shutter clips are available for invisibly mounting vinyl shutters.

Install a new storm door

Cost: $100 and up; door shown, about $400
Time: 2 to 4 hours

Even if your primary door remains the same, a storm door with an oval window or decorative glass can act as a great cover-up. It can add security and increase your home's energy efficiency.

Self-storing units with glass and screen panels that can be adjusted in tracks according to season are the most convenient. Those with interchangeable screens and storm panels have a cleaner, uninterrupted look but require a safe place to store the unused panel.

Install flower boxes

Cost: $20 to $30 each
Time: 1 hour to install store-bought boxes; 3 to 4 hours to build and install your own

Few projects add as much charm and color to a house as flowers planted in window boxes. These work best when mounted below double-hung, slide-by or stationary windows—casement and other swing-out window sashes will decapitate the flowers. Use a plastic liner to prolong the life of the planter and simplify fall cleanup.

Easier yet, arrange container gardens in pots and planters on the front stoop or along the walkway.

71 Make over your kitchen cabinets

Loose door hinges

Misaligned doors

Door won't latch

Stained cutting board

Loose knobs

Worn-out door slides

Sticking drawers

Loud doors

Nicks and scratches

Broken drawer box

1

CUTTING BOARD

KOSHER SALT

Mineral Oil

2

Clean a yucky cutting board

If you love the convenience of your pullout wooden cutting board but don't use it because it's stained and grungy, try this chef-approved, two-step process. Simply scour the board with a lemon and a pile of kosher salt, then apply mineral oil. The coarse kosher salt is an excellent abrasive, and the citric acid kills bacteria. When the stains are gone, rinse the board and let it dry. Mineral oil helps prevent the wood from absorbing stains.

1 Scour the cutting board with a lemon and kosher salt until the board is clean.

2 Apply mineral oil to the board and wipe off the excess. After a few hours, apply a second coat.

Adjust hinges on misaligned doors

If your cabinet doors are out of whack and you have European-style hinges, you're in luck. Euro hinges are designed for easy adjustment. Don't let their complex look scare you; all you have to do is turn a few screws, and any mistakes you make are easy to correct. The Euro hinge shown here adjusts in three directions. Others adjust in two directions. Either way, it's a trial-and-error process: You make adjustments, close the door to check the fit, then adjust again until it's right.

First: If the door isn't flush with the doors next to it, adjust the **depth screw**. This screw moves the door in or out. Some depth screws move the door as you turn them. But with most, you have to loosen the screw, nudge the door in or out and then tighten the screw. If your hinges don't have depth screws, start with the side screws.

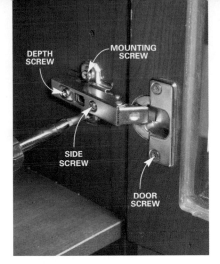

DEPTH SCREW — MOUNTING SCREW — SIDE SCREW — DOOR SCREW

1 Tighten the door screws and the mounting screws before you make any adjustments. Then adjust the depth screw and side screw.

Second: If the door is crooked—not standing parallel to adjacent doors or square with the cabinet—adjust the **side screw**. This moves the door from side to side. In some cases, you have to loosen the depth screw slightly to adjust the side screw.

2 Check the fit of the door after each adjustment. With double doors like these, perfect the fit of one door first, then align the other door.

Third: If the door is flush and parallel with other doors but too high or low, use the **mounting screws** to raise or lower the mounting plates. Loosen the screws at both hinges, slide the door up or down and tighten the screws. Some mounting plates adjust by turning a single screw.

Adjust or replace bad latches

Most newer cabinets have self-closing hinges that hold the doors shut. Others have magnetic or roller catches. A catch that no longer keeps a door closed is either broken or out of adjustment. Catches are fastened with two screws, so replacing a damaged catch is simple, and it costs less than $2. Adjustment is just as simple, but you might have to readjust the catch a couple of times before you get it right. Loosen the screws, move the catch in or out, and tighten the screws. If the door doesn't close tightly, try again.

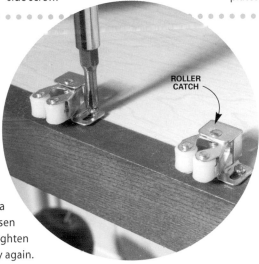

ROLLER CATCH

tip If you have a door that's slightly warped and won't lie flat against the cabinet, try adding a magnetic catch at the trouble spot. Often the magnet is strong enough to pull the door in tight.

Add bumpers to banging doors

Tired of listening to those cabinet doors bang shut? Peel-and-stick door and drawer bumpers are the solution. Get a pack of 20 at a home center for $2. Make sure the back of the door is clean so the bumpers will stick, then place one at the top corner and another at the bottom.

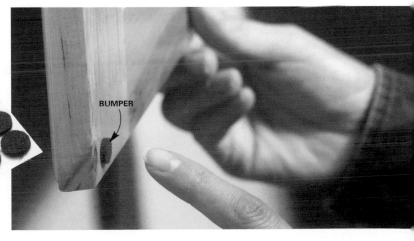

BUMPER

Replace worn-out drawer slides

If you find that slides are bent, or rollers are broken or won't turn even after lubricating, replacement is the best solution. To keep the project simple, buy new slides that are identical (or almost identical) to the old ones. That way, replacement is an easy matter of unscrewing the old and screwing on the new. Remove a drawer track and a cabinet track and take them shopping with you. Whether you have pairs of side-mounted slides (as shown here) or single, center-mount slides, there's a good chance you'll find very similar slides at a home center for $5 to $15 per drawer. If you can't find them, check with a cabinet materials supplier.

Lubricate sticking drawers

A few minutes of cleaning and lubricating can make drawer slides glide almost like new. Start by removing the drawers so you can inspect the slides. You can remove most drawers by pulling them all the way out, then either lifting or lowering the front of the drawer until the wheels come out of the track. Wipe the tracks clean and coat them with a light spray lubricant. Also lubricate the rollers and make sure they spin easily.

Repair a broken drawer box

Don't put up with a broken corner joint on a drawer. Fix it before the whole drawer comes apart. Remove the drawer and then remove the drawer front from the drawer box, if possible. Most fronts are fastened by a couple of screws inside the box. Wood glue will make a strong repair if there's wood-to-wood contact at the joint. If the wood at the joint is coated, use epoxy instead of wood glue.

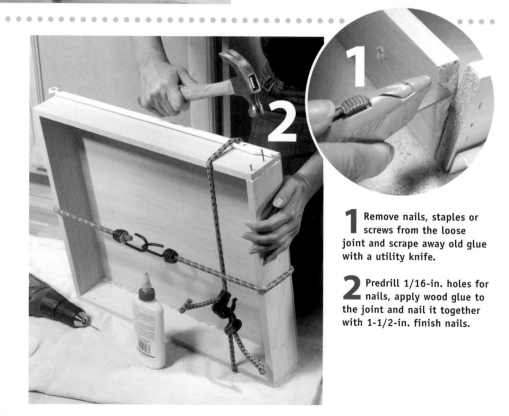

1 Remove nails, staples or screws from the loose joint and scrape away old glue with a utility knife.

2 Predrill 1/16-in. holes for nails, apply wood glue to the joint and nail it together with 1-1/2-in. finish nails.

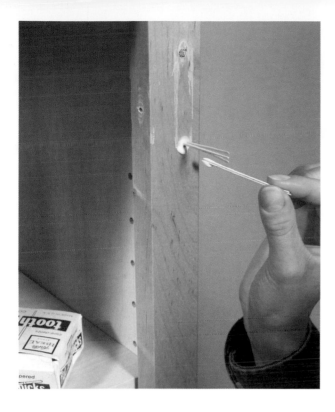

FILLER PENCIL

Fill stripped screw holes

When cabinet doors, catches or drawer slides aren't working right, step one is to make sure the screws are tight. If a screw turns but doesn't tighten, the screw hole is stripped. Here's a quick remedy:

Remove the screw and hardware. Dip toothpicks in glue, jam as many as you can into the hole and break them off. Either flat or round toothpicks will work. If you don't have toothpicks handy, shave splinters off a wood scrap with a utility knife. Immediately wipe away glue drips with a damp cloth. You don't have to wait for the glue to dry or drill new screw holes; just go ahead and reinstall the hardware by driving screws right into the toothpicks.

Touch up nicks and scratches

If you have shallow scratches or nicks, hide them with a stain-filled touch-up marker. Dab on the stain and wipe off the excess with a rag. But beware: Scratches can absorb lots of stain and turn darker than the surrounding finish. So start with a marker that's lighter than your cabinet finish and then switch to a darker shade if needed. For deeper scratches, use a filler pencil, which fills and colors the scratch. If the cabinet finish is dingy overall and has lots of scratches, consider a wipe-on product like Old English Scratch Coat. These products can darken the finish slightly, so you have to apply them to all of your cabinets.

Glue loose knobs

Any handle or knob that comes loose once is likely to come loose again. Put a permanent stop to this problem with a tiny drop of thread adhesive like Thread Lok (about $3 at home centers). Don't worry; if you want to replace your hardware sometime in the future, the knobs will still come off with a screwdriver.

Buyer's Guide

All the cabinet hardware and products mentioned here are available at home centers and hardware stores. For a larger selection of hinges, catches and drawer slides, check out Woodworker's Hardware at (800) 383-0130, www.wwhardware.com.

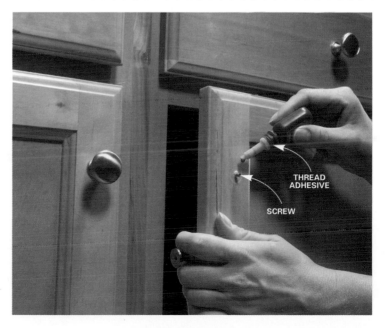

THREAD ADHESIVE

SCREW

Install a rock-solid stair rail

72

Would your stair rail hold up to three energetic kids hanging on it? If you're not sure, or if you have stairways with missing rails, now's the time to fix the problem. More accidents happen on stairways than anywhere else in the house, and a strong stair rail goes a long way toward making stairs safer and easier to use.

Here you'll learn how to cut and assemble your rail and how to mount it solidly to the wall framing. The design slightly exceeds the building codes in many regions. The railing extends beyond both the top and the bottom steps. While this isn't always possible, it allows you to grasp the railing sooner and hold on longer to maintain good balance.

Before you go shopping for your rail, measure from the nosing of the top landing to the floor at the bottom of the stairs and add 2 ft. This is the length of rail material you'll need. You'll find code-approved handrail and the other materials you'll need at lumberyards and home centers. Expect to spend about $5 per linear foot for an oak rail like the one shown here. Pine and poplar rails cost less. In addition to the rail, you'll need handrail brackets

(Photo 11, p. 97), a package of two-part, 90-second epoxy, and about 4 ft. of 2x4. Buy enough brackets to install two at the top, one at the bottom and one every 48 in. between the top and the bottom.

Locate and mark the studs

In order to be safe, stair rails must be anchored securely to the wood framing behind the drywall or plaster. Here are a few tips for locating the studs. Start by inspecting the skirt board to see if you can detect a pattern of nails that may indicate studs. Then use a stud finder to verify the locations. Most studs are 16 in. on center, so once you find one, you can try measuring horizontally to locate the next one. When you find a stud, mark it with a strip of masking tape (Photo 1). Scotch Safe-Release masking tape is a good choice to avoid damaging the paint or wallpaper. Mark every stud along the stairs plus one beyond the top and bottom risers. You'll decide later which ones to use. Studs aren't always where you want them. If no stud is available at the top, use metal toggle anchors to mount the bracket under the short horizontal section of rail. If there's no room to extend the handrail past the top or bottom steps, simply return the handrail to the wall.

In addition to finding the studs, you have to make marks at the top and bottom of the stairway to indicate the height of the rail above the stairs. To meet building code requirements, the rail should be mounted so that the top is 34 to 38 in. above the front edge of the stair nosings. Photo 2 shows how to find this point at the top of the stair. Repeat the process on the bottom step. Later you'll align the top of the rail with these marks and locate the rail brackets (Photo 7). Then you'll use the mark at the top to position the rail before you attach it to the brackets (Photo 7 inset).

Use the stairs as a rail pattern

Cut the rail and glue on the short horizontal section at the top. Since the rail runs parallel to the stairs, you can use the stair noses as a guide for cutting the rail to the right length and for figuring the top angle (Photos 3 – 5).

Start by cutting a 45-degree angle on one end of the rail. This cut is for the short return to the wall. Rest the cut end on the floor and mark the top (Photo 3). Cut 16-degree angles on the rail and short horizontal sections. This is an approximate angle. You'll test the fit. Trim the cuts until you get a tight fit (Photos 4 and 5). Don't worry if you lose a little length on the rail. It'll just reduce the distance the rail extends at the bottom, which isn't critical. When you're satisfied with the fit, cut the short horizontal rail section to length with a 45-degree miter on the end. Make it long enough to extend a few inches past the next stud so you can add a handrail bracket under it.

1

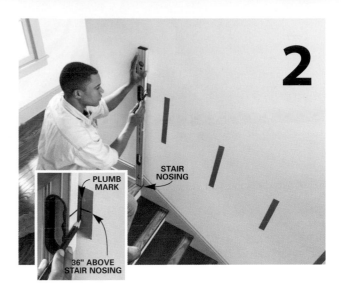

2

1 Locate the studs in the wall above the stairs. Use a stud finder and mark the locations with strips of 1-1/2-in. masking tape centered about 36 in. above the stairs.

2 Plumb up from the front edge of the top stair nosing and stick a piece of tape to the wall. Make a vertical line even with the front of the nosing and a horizontal line at 36 in. Do the same at the bottom tread.

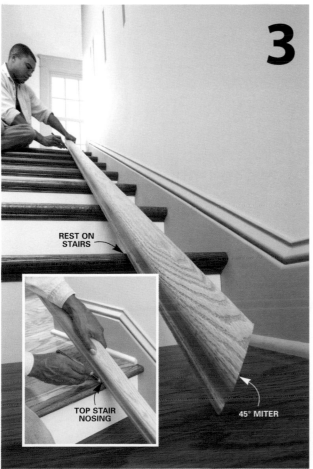

3

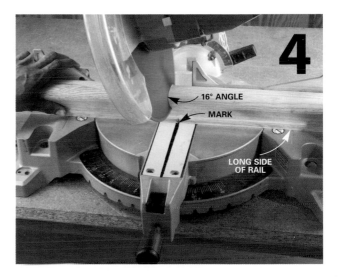

4

3 Cut a 45-degree miter on one end of the rail and rest this end on the floor. With the rail resting on the front of the stair treads, mark where the rail contacts the top stair nosing (see inset photo).

4 Set your power miter saw to cut a 16-degree angle and saw the rail at the mark. Cut the opposite 16-degree angle on the remaining rail piece. Use it for the horizontal top section.

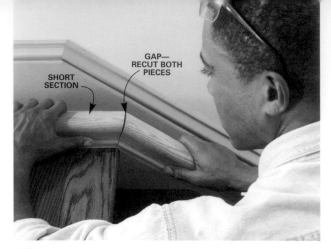

5 Test the fit of the rail joint. Adjust the cutting angle and recut both pieces until the joint is tight. Then cut a 45-degree miter on the other end of the short piece, allowing enough length to reach the next stud.

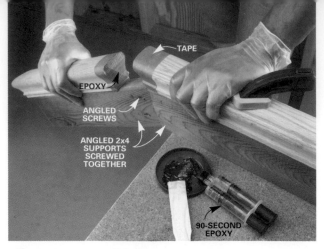

6 Mix 90-second epoxy for 30 seconds, apply a thin layer to the end of both rail sections, and press and hold the pieces together for one minute until the epoxy starts to set. Carefully remove the protective masking tape after about five minutes. Let the epoxy harden for at least two hours.

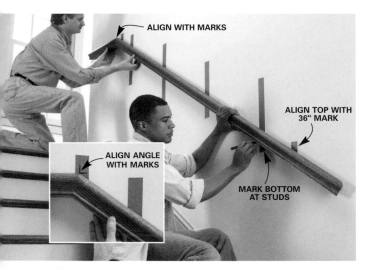

7 Align the top of the handrail with the 36-in.-high marks on the tape (see inset photo), and mark along the underside of the rail at each stud location.

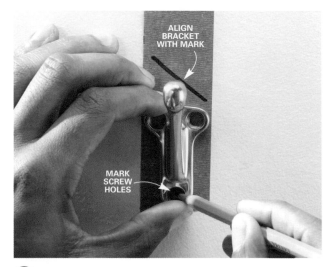

8 Center the rail bracket vertically on the stud and sight across the top to align it with the mark. Then mark all three screw holes. Do this at the studs closest to the top and bottom of the rail.

The shallow angle makes it difficult to join the short and long rail sections with nails or screws. And dowels or other joining methods require a furniture maker's precision. Instead, a simple method shown here joins the two with fast-setting epoxy. Cut 2x4s on edge at the same angle as the rail and join them with screws driven at an angle (Photo 6). Then support the rail sections with the 2x4s as you press and hold the joint together. With 90-second epoxy, you'll be able to hand-hold the joint together long enough for the epoxy to grab. Concentrate on keeping the profiles exactly lined up and pressing the rails tight together to eliminate gaps. Then leave the joint undisturbed for at least an hour. Overnight would be better, since the epoxy doesn't approach maximum strength for at least 24 hours. To protect the wood from epoxy that may ooze out, wrap the rail ends with masking tape (Photo 6). Trim excess tape flush to the cut end with a sharp utility knife. Then carefully remove the tape after the epoxy has set for five minutes. The finished joint will probably require sanding to even up the edges. Do this after the epoxy hardens.

Locate and mount the brackets

Photos 7 and 8 show how to mark the underside of the handrail at the stud locations and how to use these marks to align and attach the rail brackets. Position and install two brackets first, one close to the top and one close to the bottom of the rail. Photo 9 shows how to locate the exact center of the studs. This is an important step because the rail brackets must be centered on the stud or one of the two top screws will miss the framing. Shift the bracket slightly if necessary to center it on the stud. If you shift the bracket, make sure to adjust the height to keep the top aligned with the mark (Photo 8). You may have to patch a few nail holes, but this beats having a bracket pull loose. Install the top and bottom brackets first and mount the rail to them (Photo 12). Then add the bracket under the short horizontal section. Finally, sight down the rail and straighten it before adding the intermediate brackets.

Be careful when you drive the screws included with the brackets. The heads will break off easily if you don't predrill pilot holes. If you're driving the screws with a drill, mount the bit in a magnetic bit holder to extend it away from the drill.

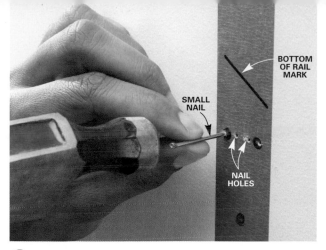

9 Probe the wall with a finish nail to locate the exact center of the stud. Tap gently to feel when the nail hits solid wood or misses the stud and goes in easily. Shift the bracket if necessary until there's solid wood behind both top holes.

BOTTOM OF RAIL MARK

SMALL NAIL

NAIL HOLES

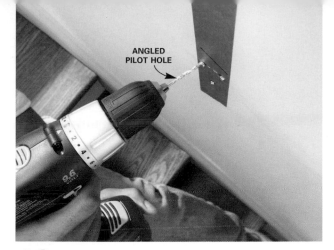

10 Drill 1/8-in. pilot holes for the rail bracket screws. You should feel the bit drilling into solid wood. Angle holes slightly toward the center to make sure the screws catch the stud.

ANGLED PILOT HOLE

11 Remove the masking tape and screw the bracket to the wall. Angle the top screws slightly to follow the angled pilot holes.

MAGNETIC BIT EXTENSION

ANGLE BRACKET SCREW

RAIL BRACKET

U-SHAPED BRACKET

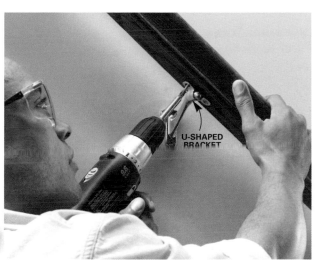

12 Set the rail on the two brackets and align the top joint with the marks on the tape. Drill pilot holes and then attach the rail to the brackets with the screws and strap provided. Install additional brackets.

U-SHAPED BRACKET

Add the returns to complete the rail

With the rail mounted, it's easy to measure for and install the short pieces that return to the wall at the top and bottom of the rail (Photo 13). Measure from the long point of the 45-degree miter on the rail to the wall and add about 1/16 in. for a tight fit. Then cut the returns on your power miter saw. Cut them from longer pieces (at least 12 in.) to avoid getting your fingers too close to the blade. These returns are required by the building code, and for good reason. They eliminate the possibility that loose clothing or a purse strap could get hung up and cause a fall. Besides, they create a nice finished look on the ends of the rail. Attach the returns with wood glue and 4d finish nails, or use the remaining 90-second epoxy. Once the rail is complete, you can take it off to paint or finish it by simply removing the screws from the U-shaped brackets. Since the screw holes are already drilled, it'll be easy to reinstall.

13 Cut the short returns on your miter saw. Predrill 1/16-in. holes, then glue and tack the joint with 4d finish nails. Recess the nails with a nail set.

MITERED RETURN

WOOD GLUE

4d FINISH NAILS

73 Convert wood cabinet doors to glass

A pair of glass doors can add a designer touch to any kitchen. They can turn an ordinary cabinet into a decorative showcase or simply break up an otherwise monotonous row of solid doors. This alteration is for frame-and-panel cabinet doors only (see Figure A), where you can replace the inset wood panels with glass. Converting the two doors shown here takes about two hours.

To get started, remove the doors from the cabinets and remove all hardware from the doors. Examine the back side of each door; you might find a few tiny nails where the panel meets the frame. If so, gouge away wood with a utility knife to expose the nail heads and pull the nails with a pliers. Look carefully; just one leftover nail will chip your expensive router bit.

Cut away the lips using a router and a 1/2-in. pattern bit (Photo 1). A pattern bit ($25) is simply a straight bit equipped with a bearing that rolls along a guide. Most home centers and hardware stores don't carry pattern bits. To find a retailer, check the yellow pages under "Woodworking" or order one at www.pricecutter.com (888-288-2487). Be sure to choose a bit that has the bearing on the top, not at the bottom.

Use any straight, smooth material (solid wood, plywood or MDF) to make two 3-1/2-in.-wide guides. To allow for the 1-in. cutting depth of the pattern bit, nail layers of plywood and MDF together to make 1-3/8-in.-thick guides. Position the guides 1/2 in. from the inner edges of the lips and clamp them firmly in place over the door. Support the outer edges of the guides with strips of wood that match the thickness of the door to keep them level (Photo 1). Before you start routing, make sure the door itself is clamped firmly in place.

Set the router on the guide and adjust the cutting depth so that the bit just touches the panel. Cut away the lips on two sides, then reposition the guides to cut away the other two. With the lips removed, lift the panel out of the frame. If the panel is stuck, a few light hammer taps will free it.

If your door frame has a rectangular opening, it's now ready for glass. If it has an arched upper rail, cut a square recess above the arch (Photo 2). This allows you to use a rectangular

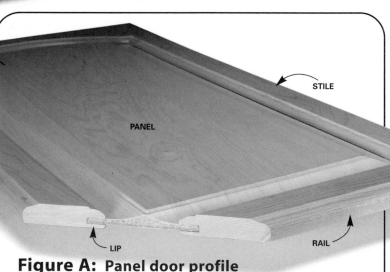

Figure A: Panel door profile

Most cabinet doors are made like this one: A raised or flat panel fits into grooves in the rails-and-stile frame. To remove the panel, just cut away the lips on the back side of the door.

1 Clamp router guides to the back side of the door. Run a pattern bit along the guides to cut away the inside lips.

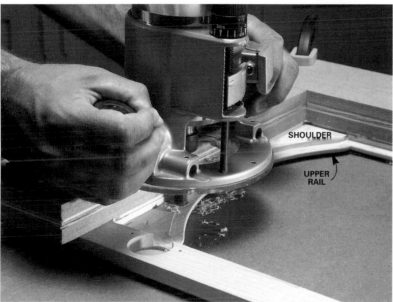

2 Lower the router bit and cut away the shoulders on the back side of an arched upper rail to create a square recess for the glass.

3 Set the glass into the frame and secure it with glass clips placed no more than 12 in. apart. Then reinstall the doors.

Glass doors can turn an ordinary cabinet into a decorative showcase

piece of glass rather than a curved piece (curved cuts are expensive). Then simply lay the glass in and anchor it with glass clips (Photo 3). Clips are available from the glass supplier or at www.woodworkershardware.com, (800-383-0130; item No. LAH264; $4 for 20 clips).

If the glass rattles in the frame, add pea-size blobs of hot-melt glue every 12 in.

Buying glass

Most hardware stores carry clear glass ($3 per sq. ft.) and will cut it for free or a small fee. Ask for 3/16-in.-thick "double strength" glass. Order glass panels 1/8 in. smaller than the recess in the frame. To find tempered, textured or colored glass ($5 to $15 per sq. ft.), check the yellow pages under "Glass." You can buy clear textured glass and pay a supplier an extra $60 or so to have the panels tempered. Building codes require tempered glass for locations within 5 ft. of the floor.

⁊₄ Organize your garage for less than $200

There are lots of ways to create more storage space in your garage, but you won't find another system that's as simple, inexpensive or versatile as this one. It begins with a layer of plywood fastened over drywall or bare studs. Then you just screw on a variety of hooks, hangers, shelves and baskets to suit your needs. That's it. The plywood base lets you quickly mount any kind of storage hardware in any spot—no searching for studs. And because you can place hardware wherever you want (not only at studs), you can arrange items close together to make the most of your wall space. As your needs change, you'll appreciate the versatility of this storage wall too; just unscrew shelves or hooks to rearrange the whole system.

Shown here are three types of storage hardware: wire shelves, wire baskets, and a variety of hooks, hangers and brackets. Selecting and arranging these items to suit your stuff can be the most time-consuming part of this project. To simplify that task, outline the dimensions of your plywood wall on the garage floor with masking tape. Then gather all the stuff you want to store and lay it out on your outline. Arrange and rearrange items to make the most of your wall space. Then make a list of the hardware you need before you head off to the hardware store or home center.

Money, materials and planning

The total materials bill for the 6 x 16-ft. section of wall shown here was about $200. Everything you need is available at home centers. You can use 3/4-in.-thick "BC" grade plywood, which has one side sanded smooth ($27 per 4 x 8-ft. sheet) or save a few bucks by using 3/4-in. OSB "chip board" (oriented-strand board; $16 per sheet) or MDF (medium-density fiberboard; $23 per sheet). But don't use particleboard; it doesn't hold screws well enough for this job. Aside from standard hand tools, all you need to complete this project is a drill to drive screws and a circular saw to cut plywood. You may also need a helper when handling plywood—full sheets are awkward and heavy.

This project doesn't require much planning; just decide how much of the wall you want to cover with plywood. You can cover an entire wall floor-to-ceiling or cover any section of a wall. Here, the lower 3 ft. of wall and upper 18 in. are left uncovered, since those high and low areas are best used for other types of storage. To make the most of the plywood, combine a course of full-width sheets with a course of sheets cut in half. If your ceiling height is 9 ft. or less, a single 4-ft.-wide course of plywood may suit your needs.

Cover the wall with plywood

When you've determined the starting height of the plywood, measure up from the floor at one end of the wall and drive a nail. Then measure down to the nail from the ceiling and use that measurement to make a pencil mark at the other end of the wall. (Don't measure up from the floor, since garage floors often slope.) Hook your chalk line on the nail, stretch it to the pencil mark and snap a line (Photo 1).

Cut the first sheet of plywood to length so it ends at the

7' TO CEILING

2'

STUD LOCATION

CHALK LINE

2-1/4" SCREW

SUPPORT BLOCK

1 Snap a level chalk line to mark the bottom edge of the plywood. Locate studs and mark them with masking tape.

2 Screw temporary blocks to studs at the chalk line. Start a few screws in the plywood. Rest the plywood on the blocks and screw it to studs.

Storage supplies for every need

Wire closet shelves are sturdy and inexpensive, and they don't collect dust like solid shelving. They come in lengths up to 12 ft. and you can cut them to any length using a hacksaw or bolt cutters. Standard depths are 12, 16 and 20 in. A 12-in. x 12-ft. shelf costs about $10. You'll get more shelving for your money by cutting up long sections than by buying shorter sections. Brackets and mounting clips (Photo 4) are usually sold separately.

Wire baskets are perfect for items that won't stay put on shelves (like balls and other toys) and for bags of charcoal or fertilizer that tend to tip and spill. They're also convenient because they're mobile; hang them on hooks and you can lift them off to tote all your tools or toys to the garden or sandbox. You'll find baskets in a variety of shapes and sizes at home centers and discount stores. The large baskets shown here cost about $10 each. You can use just about any type of hook to hang baskets. Heavy-duty mirror supports fit these baskets perfectly.

Hooks, hangers and brackets handle all the odd items that don't fit on shelves or in baskets. Basic hooks ($1 to $4) are often labeled for a specific purpose, but you can use them in other ways. Big "ladder brackets," for example, can hold several long-handled tools. "Ceiling hooks" for bikes also work on walls. Don't write off the wall area below the plywood—it's prime space for items that don't protrude far from the wall. To hang an extension ladder, drive hooks into the studs.

MIRROR SUPPORT HOOK

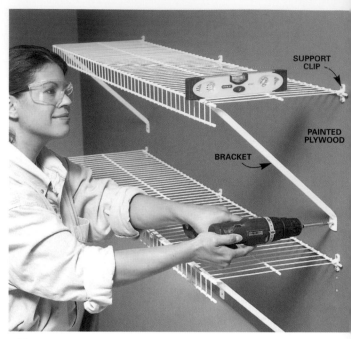

3 Set the upper course of plywood in place and screw it to studs. Stagger the vertical joints between the upper and lower courses.

4 Fasten the back edge of shelves with plastic clips. Set a level on the shelf and install the end brackets. Then add center brackets every 2 ft.

center of a stud. Place the end you cut in the corner. That way the factory-cut edge will form a tight joint with the factory edge of the next sheet. Be sure to place the rough side of the plywood against the wall. Fasten the plywood with 10d finish nails or screws that are at least 2-1/4 in. long (Photo 2). Use trim screws, which have small heads that are easy to cover with a dab of spackling compound. Drive screws or nails every 12 in. into each stud. If you add a second course of plywood above the first as shown here (Photo 3), cut the plywood to width. You can use a circular saw, but a table saw gives you faster, straighter cuts. Some home centers and lumberyards cut plywood for free or for a small charge.

With all the plywood in place, you could go ahead and mount your hardware, or take a few extra steps to dress up the wall: First, consider adding 3/4-in. cove molding along the lower edge of the plywood. This will give you a neater look and cover up the chalk line and screw holes left by the support blocks. Also frame the window trim with doorstop molding to hide small gaps between the trim and the plywood. Then caulk gaps between the sheets of plywood and fill screw holes. Finally, prime the plywood, lightly sand it with 100-grit sandpaper and paint it.

Now's the time to add outlets

The National Electrical Code requires only one outlet in a garage—and a single outlet is all most builders install.

If your garage has bare stud walls, adding outlets is easy anytime. But if your walls are covered, our plywood storage wall makes adding outlets or extra circuits easier because you can cut big holes in the drywall to run wire and cover up the damage with the plywood. No patching needed. Since the plywood itself will be covered with shelves and hangers, place new outlets below it for easier access. If you have an existing outlet that will be covered with plywood, cut a hole in the plywood about 1/8 in. larger than the junction box and add a box extender (see photo). All garage outlets must be either GFCI outlets or connected to a circuit that's GFCI-protected, so you may need to replace your existing outlet with a GFCI version.

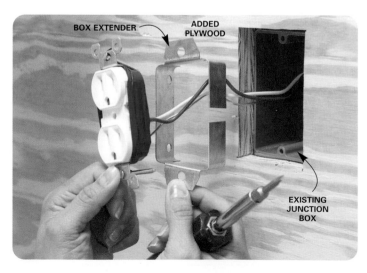

5 Acrylic photo frames make great label holders. Just slip in your labels and hot glue the frames to wire baskets. Frames cost about $2 each at office supply and discount stores.

Handy hooks

When you're out shopping, you might find elaborate hangers designed to hold specific toys and tools. These specialty hooks are neat, but you don't have to spend $10 or more just to hang a bike or garden tools. With a little ingenuity, you can hang just about anything on simple screw-in hooks that typically cost about $1 each. You can place hooks anywhere on your plywood wall. If you don't put them on the plywood, be sure to locate them at studs.

Drill a hole at a 45-degree angle and turn in a screw hook to hang a bicycle by the front wheel.

Hang ladders on hooks below the plywood for easy access.

75 Add more kitchen storage

Chances are, your kitchen has plenty of storage space—it's just that a good chunk of it is hidden in the hard-to-get-at corners, nooks and crannies of your cabinets. Deep base cabinets and corner cabinets pose particular problems.

Here you'll find five projects that create more storage space and make existing cabinet space more accessible. Each project is constructed using readily available lumber, plywood, hardware, L-moldings, glue and screws. For speed and accuracy, use a power miter saw. You can do any of these five projects in a Saturday morning. If you want to do them all, start with the easiest and end with the hardest so if you're a beginner, you can build your do-it-yourself skills and confidence as you work your way through.

Since many cabinet openings differ in height and width, the how-to steps concentrate on basic "key measurements" rather than exact dimensions.

tip Some of these projects mount to cabinet doors or face frames. Make sure your cabinets, doors and hinges are in good shape, and don't overload the finished projects with heavy cans and other weighty objects.

Door-mounted spice rack p. 106

Glide-out and swing-out shelves p. 108

Swing-down cookbook rack p. 105

Door-mounted lid rack p. 106

Roll-out pantry cabinet p. 110

Swing-down cookbook rack

When counter space is at a minimum and counter mess at a maximum, this swing-down rack will keep your cookbook up and out of the fray. The special spring-loaded brackets allow you to swing your cookbook down when you need it, then out of the way when you're done.

This cookbook platform tucks under a single cabinet. But you can make your platform larger to hold larger books, then mount it beneath two cabinets. With a little creativity, you can use this same hardware to create a swing-down knife rack or spice rack too.

Fold-down brackets are available from Kitchen Organizers (The Hardware Hut; 800-708-6649; www.kitchen-organizers.com).

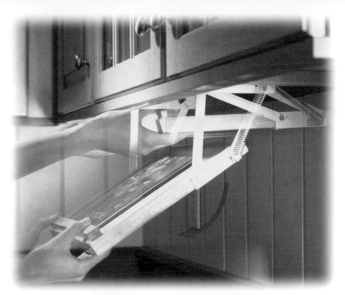

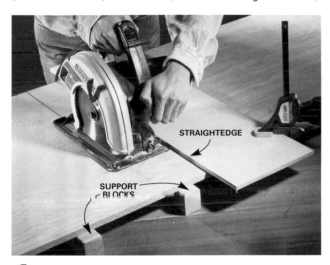

1 Cut the 1/2-in.-thick plywood base to size. To get straight cuts, measure from the edge of the circular saw base to the edge of the blade, then clamp a straight board to the plywood that distance from your cutting line to serve as a guide. Cut with the plywood's "good" side down.

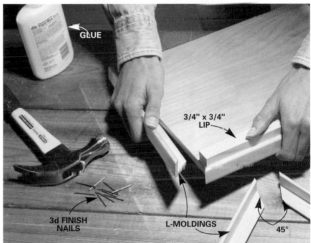

2 Glue and nail the 3/4- x 3/4-in. lip to the front of the base, then "picture frame" the plywood with L-moldings. For an exact measurement, cut one end at 45 degrees on a miter saw, hold it in position and mark the other end. Put a "reminder mark" on the board to help remember which direction to cut the angle. Secure the pieces with wood glue and 3d nails.

Figure A
Swing-down cookbook rack

MACHINE BOLT WITH WASHER AND LOCK NUT

PLYWOOD

3/4" x 3/4" LIP

3d FINISH NAIL

1" x 1" L-MOLDINGS

SWING-DOWN HINGES

■ Overall dimensions can vary according to space available

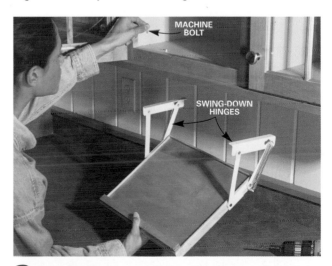

3 Mount the hinges to your base using wood screws. Hold the assembled unit in position under the cabinet, then mark the holes for the brackets (a two-person job). Drill the holes, then secure the brackets to the cabinet using short machine screws, washers and nuts.

Door-mounted spice and lid racks

These simple racks will help transform those chaotic gangs of spice bottles and pan lids into orderly regiments. Here you'll learn how to build only the spice rack; the lid rack uses the same steps but without the shelves. Each spice rack can hold 20 to 30 bottles, and each lid rack two to six lids, depending on the height and width of your cabinet doors. Before building, measure your spice bottles and lids to determine the spacing of your shelves and dowels. Here are other key measurements and clearances to keep an eye on:

Existing shelf depth. If the existing cabinet shelves are full depth, narrow them by about 2 in. to accommodate each door-mounted rack. Shelves that are permanently affixed in grooves in the cabinet sides will need to be cut in place with a jigsaw. Adjustable shelves can be removed, cut along the back side with a circular saw or table saw, then replaced. You may need to move brackets or add holes to remount narrowed shelves.

Spice rack depth and positioning. Make certain the new rack won't hit the cabinet frame when the door swings. Fitting the rack between the two 2-in.-wide vertical stiles (Photo 1) gives

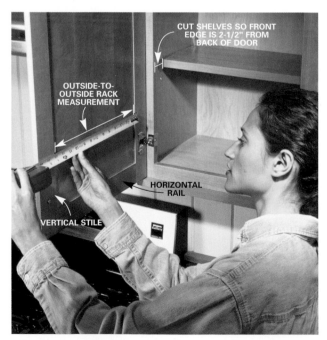

1 Measure the distance between the two vertical stiles and the two horizontal rails to determine the outside dimensions of your spice rack. Cut existing shelves back 2-1/2 in. so they don't interfere with the rack when the door is closed.

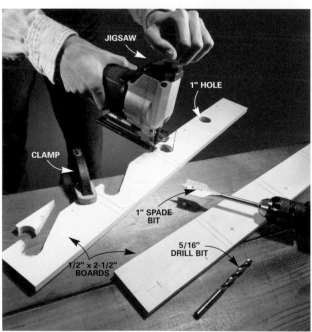

2 Transfer the dimensions from Figure B onto 1/2- x 2-1/2-in. side boards. Cut out the sides of the spice rack. Drill 1-in. holes to create the circular shape, then finish the cutout with a jigsaw. Drill 5/16-in. holes for the dowels. Sand the edges and surfaces smooth.

adequate room. If your doors are solid wood or laminate, hold in place a scrap of wood the same depth as the spice rack (2-1/2 in. was the depth on the cabinets shown) and swing the door. Move it away from the door edge until it no longer makes contact with the cabinet frame, then mark the door. This will determine the overall width of your spice rack.

You can use soft, easy-to-nail pine and basswood for both the spice and the lid racks. If you're using a harder wood, like maple or oak, position the pieces, then pre-drill holes through the side pieces and into the shelf ends. This will prevent splitting and make nailing easier. Install your shelves one at a time so you don't have to balance and juggle multiple pieces as you work. Always nail on a flat, solid surface.

tip Use high-gloss polyurethane for natural wood, high-gloss enamel for painted wood. These finishes are more "scrubbable."

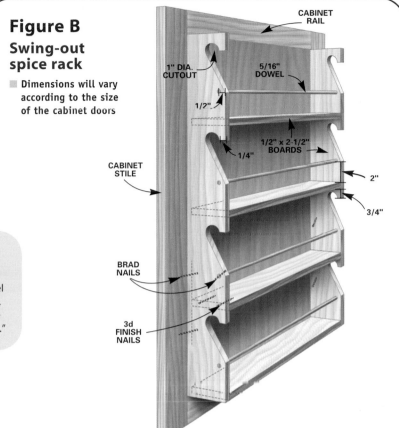

Figure B
Swing-out spice rack
▪ Dimensions will vary according to the size of the cabinet doors

CABINET RAIL
1" DIA. CUTOUT
5/16" DOWEL
1/2"
1/2" x 2-1/2" BOARDS
1/4"
2"
3/4"
CABINET STILE
BRAD NAILS
3d FINISH NAILS

1/2" x 2-1/2" SHELVES
3/4" BRAD
5/16" DOWELS

3 Glue and nail the shelves in place one at a time, using 3d finish nails. Then use 3/4-in. brads to pin the dowels in place. Sink all nail heads using a nail set. Apply polyurethane or other finish to match the cabinets.

1/16" DRILL BIT
CLAMP

4 Clamp the finished rack to the door, then drill angled pilot holes through the rack and into the door every 8 in. Secure with brad nails (remove the door for this step if a more solid surface is needed for hammering). Use wood glue for a more permanent installation.

Blind corner glide-out and swing-out shelves

Blind-corner cabinets—those with a blank face that allows another cabinet to butt into them—may be great for aging wine, but they're darn near impossible

tip Test-fit the shelf units in the cabinet as they're built.

to see and reach into. This pair of accessories puts an end to this hidden wasteland. The hinged shelf swings out of the way, and the gliding shelf slides forward so you can access food items stored in the back. You can use the same hardware and techniques for making base cabinets more accessible too.

The key measurements and clearances:

Glide-out shelf dimensions. You can only make the unit as long as the door opening is wide (or else you can't fit it in!). Make the unit about 1/2 in. narrower than the inside width of the cabinet.

Swing-out tray dimensions. The corner-to-corner or diagonal measurement of the unit (Figure C) can't exceed the width of the door opening (or else that won't fit either!). Make the unit about 1 in. shorter than the opening height so it has room to swing freely when installed.

Piano hinges (No. 19283) and bottom slides are available from Rockler (800-279-4441; www.rockler.com). The front moldings (No. 673) are manufactured by House of Fara (800-334-1732; www.houseoffara.com).

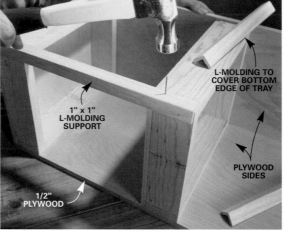

HINGED SWING-OUT SHELF

GLIDE-OUT SHELF

Build the glide-out shelf

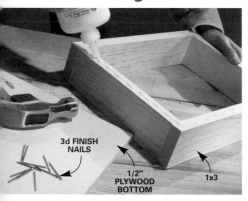

3d FINISH NAILS

1/2" PLYWOOD BOTTOM

1x3

1 Glue and nail the 1x3s together using 4d finish nails, then secure the plywood bottom with 3d finish nails.

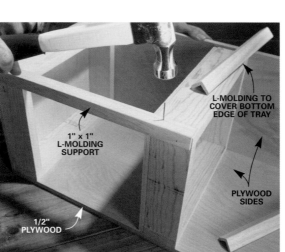

L-MOLDING TO COVER BOTTOM EDGE OF TRAY

1" x 1" L-MOLDING SUPPORT

1/2" PLYWOOD

PLYWOOD SIDES

2 Cut out the two plywood sides, then glue and nail the corners. Connect the trays to the two plywood sides using 1-in. drywall screws, then cut and nail L-molding to support the front corner. Cut and install L-moldings to support and cover the exposed plywood edges of the upper tray. Install 3/4-in. screen molding to cover the plywood edges of the bottom tray.

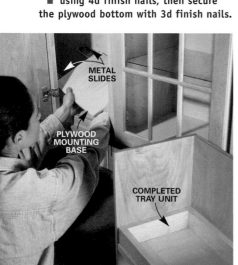

METAL SLIDES

PLYWOOD MOUNTING BASE

COMPLETED TRAY UNIT

3 Cut the mounting base plywood slightly smaller than the other tray bottoms, then secure the two slides parallel to each other about 1 in. from each edge. Slip this mounting base into the opening, extend the slides, then screw them to the cabinet bottom at the rear of the cabinet. Install the slides parallel to the cabinet sides, so the base slides back and forth freely.

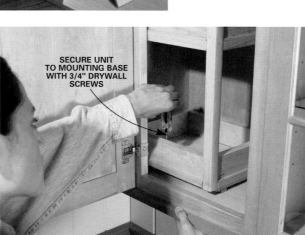

SECURE UNIT TO MOUNTING BASE WITH 3/4" DRYWALL SCREWS

4 Screw the tray unit to the mounting base using 3/4-in. screws. After installing the first screw, slide the unit forward and back, then adjust it until it runs parallel to the cabinet sides and install three more screws.

Figure C
Glide-out and swing-out shelves

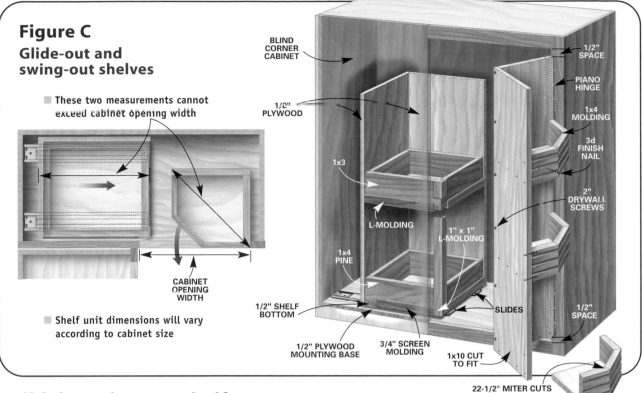

■ These two measurements cannot exceed cabinet opening width

BLIND CORNER CABINET

1/2" PLYWOOD

1x3

L-MOLDING

1x4 PINE

1/2" SHELF BOTTOM

1/2" PLYWOOD MOUNTING BASE

3/4" SCREEN MOLDING

1" x 1" L-MOLDING

1x10 CUT TO FIT

SLIDES

1/2" SPACE

PIANO HINGE

1x4 MOLDING

3d FINISH NAIL

2" DRYWALL SCREWS

1/2" SPACE

22-1/2° MITER CUTS

CABINET OPENING WIDTH

■ Shelf unit dimensions will vary according to cabinet size

Build the swing-out shelf

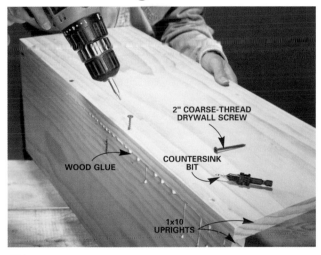

WOOD GLUE

2" COARSE-THREAD DRYWALL SCREW

COUNTERSINK BIT

1x10 UPRIGHTS

5 Cut the 1x10 swing-out uprights to length and width (one should be 3/4 in. narrower than the other). Use a countersink bit to predrill holes along one edge, then glue and screw the two edges together. The diagonal measurement (see Figure C) should be less than the cabinet opening.

6 Assemble the shelf unit. First mark the shelf positions on the uprights and predrill holes from the front side. Create the three shelves by cutting a 1x10 to length and width, then cutting the corner at 45 degrees. Hold the shelves in place and drive drywall screws through these holes from the back side into the shelves. Cut the 22-1/2-degree angles on the front moldings and secure them with 3d finish nails. Use any type of wide decorative molding that's at least 1/2 in. x 3 in.

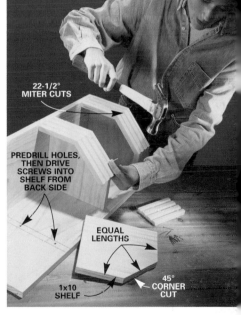

22-1/2° MITER CUTS

PREDRILL HOLES, THEN DRIVE SCREWS INTO SHELF FROM BACK SIDE

EQUAL LENGTHS

1x10 SHELF

45° CORNER CUT

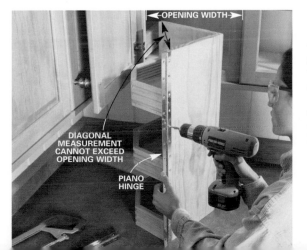

OPENING WIDTH

DIAGONAL MEASUREMENT CANNOT EXCEED OPENING WIDTH

PIANO HINGE

7 Screw the piano hinge to the front edge of the swing-out unit, then to the edge of the cabinet face frame. Make certain the swing-out has 1/2 in. of clearance top and bottom.

tip Beg, borrow or rent a compressor, finish nailer and brad gun, if possible, to work faster, eliminate hammer marks and split the wood less often than you would by hand-nailing.

Roll-out pantry cabinet

Most cabinet manufacturers now include roll-out shelves in their base cabinets. But if you don't have this convenience, this project will one-up those shelves. Here you'll learn how to make an entire roll-out pantry.

The hardware consists of two heavy-duty bottom-mounted slides and one center-mounted top slide that together can support 130 lbs. Again, construct your unit to suit your needs. The bottom tray shown here is 3-1/2 in. tall and the upper ones are 2-1/2 in. tall. You may want to include only two trays if you'll be storing cereal boxes and other tall packages.

Since you'll be converting your door from swinging to rolling mode, you'll need to remove the door and hinges. You'll also have to remove the existing handle and reinstall it centered on the door. If your hardware mounts from the back side, install it before attaching the door. Fill the holes from the old hardware location with wood putty, then sand it smooth.

The key measurements and clearances:

Roll-out unit measurements. The plywood front and back panels should be about 1/8 in. shorter than the distance between the installed top and bottom glides (Photos 1 and 2). The width of the unit should be 1/2 in. narrower than the cabi-

net opening. The depth of the unit should be 1/2 in. less than the depth of the cabinet (not including the face frame).

Accuride Pantry slides (No. 91968) are available for $83 plus shipping from Rockler (800-279-4441; www.rockler.com).

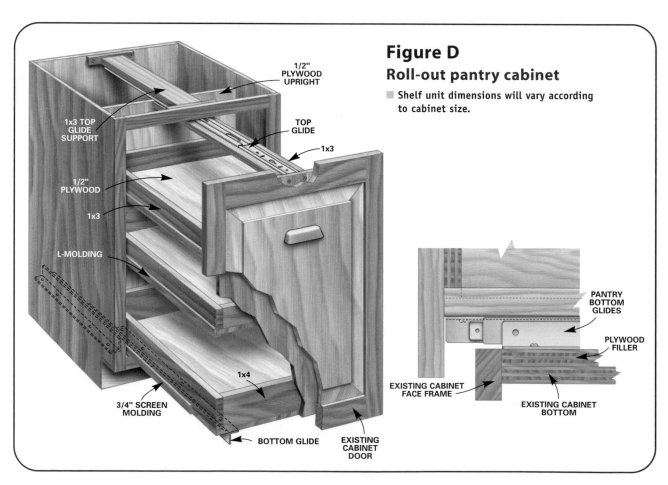

Figure D
Roll-out pantry cabinet

- Shelf unit dimensions will vary according to cabinet size.

1/2" PLYWOOD UPRIGHT

1x3 TOP GLIDE SUPPORT

TOP GLIDE

1x3

1/2" PLYWOOD

1x3

L-MOLDING

1x4

3/4" SCREEN MOLDING

BOTTOM GLIDE

EXISTING CABINET DOOR

PANTRY BOTTOM GLIDES

PLYWOOD FILLER

EXISTING CABINET FACE FRAME

EXISTING CABINET BOTTOM

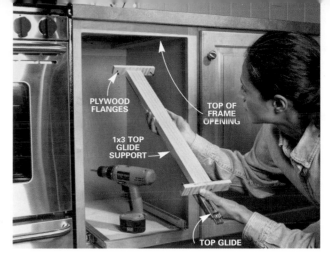

1 Measure the cabinet face frame opening, then subtract the height of the top and bottom glides. Calculate the depth, width and height of the unit. Install the bottom glides to run parallel to the cabinet sides. If necessary, use plywood to raise the cabinet bottom even with the bottom lip of the face frame.

2 Install the top glide support and top glide so the support is level and flush to the top of the frame opening. Screw plywood flanges to each end of the 1x3 support beforehand to make it simpler to secure it to the front and back of the cabinet.

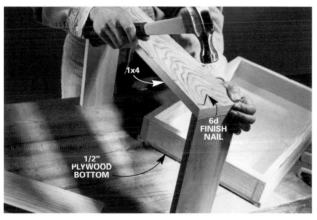

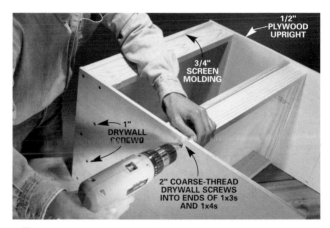

3 Assemble the pantry trays using 1x4s, 1x3s, 6d nails and wood glue. Use the plywood bottoms to "square up" the trays before nailing them on. L-moldings support and cover the plywood edges of the upper two trays; 3/4-in. screen molding covers the exposed plywood edges of the bottom tray.

4 Secure the trays to the 1/2-in. plywood uprights using glue and drywall screws. Arrange the spacing of the trays to meet your needs.

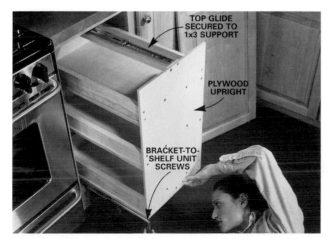

5 Screw the tray assembly to the bottom runners, making sure it's centered in the opening and running parallel to the cabinet sides. The extended portion of the top slide is secured to a 1x3 screwed between the two plywood uprights. You can loosen this 1x3, then adjust the height so the top glide runs flat and smooth.

6 Clamp the cabinet door to the front of the pantry assembly; center it and make the height even with adjacent doors. Predrill eight holes through the plywood upright and drive screws into the back of the cabinet door. After installing two screws, close the door to check its alignment with the adjacent doors. Make adjustments, then install the remaining screws. Use short screws so they don't penetrate the front of the cabinet door.

76 Give your front door a keyless lock

With friends, contractors, pet sitters and others, it's easy to lose track of extra house keys. For better control of who can get in and out—and a permanent solution to the lost-key problem with kids—replace one of your dead bolt locks with an electronic keypad entry ($100 to $200 at home centers). Instead of using a key, you just punch in a four-digit number, so you don't have to worry about being locked out. You can pick your own number and change it anytime. You can also program in additional four-digit codes for visitors, then delete them later.

Start by removing the old dead bolt (and the handle if you're replacing it). Set the new dead bolt to match the existing 2-3/8-in. or 2-3/4-in. "backset" (measured from the door edge to the center of the dead bolt hole), then install it in the deadbolt hole. Make sure that "TOP" is facing up and that the bolt is fully retracted.

Install the outside keypad first (Photo 1), then secure it in place with the inside mounting plate (Photo 2). Connect the wires to the battery and tuck them out of the way before attaching the inside cover plate (Photo 3). (Note: Shown here is a Schlage lock; other manufacturers may have different installation procedures.)

With the door open, check to make sure the dead bolt extends and retracts smoothly. If it doesn't, disassemble the lock and make sure the parts were installed correctly. To unlock the dead bolt, just punch in the code and turn the latch.

The lock shown here comes preprogrammed with two unique user codes. To change them or add more, follow the lock's programming instructions.

The lock will signal when the battery needs replacing. A key is also included in case the lock ever malfunctions or loses battery power and needs to be opened manually. One big caution: Don't lose the programming guide. It contains the user codes, programming codes and instructions for changing codes.

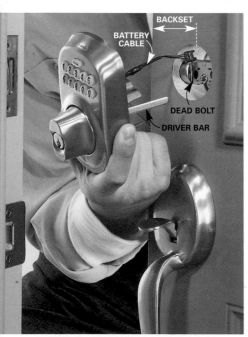

1 Hold the keypad upright and slide the battery cable over the top of the dead bolt and the driver bar through the center slot of the dead bolt.

2 Pull the battery cable through, then hold the keypad and the inside mounting plate together while you tighten the screws.

3 Hook up the battery and snap it into place, make sure the keypad and inside plate are level, then screw on the cover plate.

77 Install a **programmable thermostat**

When it comes to energy savings, few upgrades pay off as quickly as a programmable thermostat. If you turn down the heat 5 degrees at night and 10 degrees during the day when no one is home, you'll cut your energy bill by 5 to 20 percent. If you raise the temperature the same amount during the cooling season, your savings will be similar. You can do this with a manual thermostat, but a programmable model never forgets to turn down the heat at night and it can raise the temperature before you get out of bed in the morning.

Home centers carry several programmable models ranging from $25 to $100. Generally, more money means more programming options. Standard programmable thermostats sold in stores work with most heating/cooling systems, new or old. But there are exceptions: Electric baseboard heat systems require a "line voltage" thermostat that's connected to much larger wires than those shown here. Heat pumps often require special thermostats, too. If you can't find the one you need at a store, try www.thermostatshop.com. Before you shop, measure the "footprint" of the old thermostat. If you buy a new one that's at least as large, you won't be left with wallpaper gaps or paint to touch up.

Your old thermostat may look different from the one shown here, but removing it will require similar steps. Turn off the power at the main electrical panel by switching off the furnace breaker. If the furnace circuit isn't labeled, switch on the heat (not the air conditioning) and turn off breakers until the furnace stops. Remove the old thermostat (Photo 1). Chances are, it has a small glass tube containing mercury, which is toxic. Call your city or state environmental or health department for disposal instructions.

You'll find anywhere from two to six wires connected to the old thermostat. If any of them aren't connected to

1 Pull off the cover ring and remove the screws that fasten the thermostat to the wall plate.

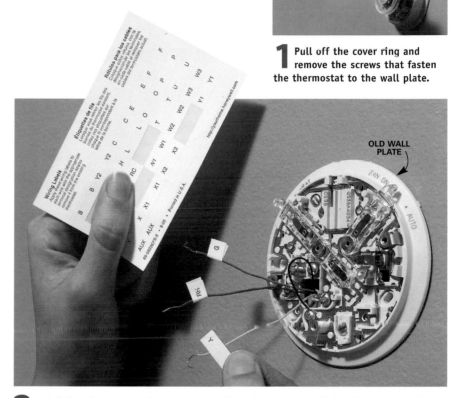

OLD WALL PLATE

2 Label the wires as you disconnect them from the screw terminals. Then remove the mounting screws that fasten the wall plate.

3 Mark the new screw locations, drive in wall anchors and screw the mounting plate to the wall. Connect the wires.

NEW WALL PLATE

4 Install the batteries, program the thermostat and snap it onto the wall plate.

the screw terminals, you won't connect them to the new thermostat either. The terminals are labeled with letters. As you remove each wire, label it to match the terminal using the tags included with the new thermostat (Photo 2). Disregard the color of the wires. When you remove the last wire, clip a clothespin to the cable so it

can't slip inside the wall.

Mount the wall plate (Photo 3). In most cases, you'll simply connect the wires by matching labels to the letters on the new wall plate, but check the manufacturer's instructions to be sure. Program and install the thermostat (Photo 4). Don't forget to turn the power back on at the main panel.

78 Install a dimmer switch

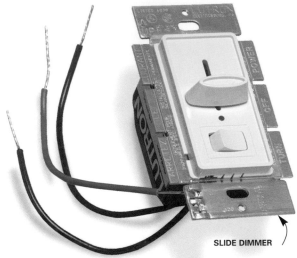

SLIDE DIMMER

It doesn't take long to replace an ordinary light switch with a full-feature dimmer. But while you're at it, to make your home safer, you should upgrade the wiring to meet the latest requirements of the National Electrical Code. These step-by-step instructions show you how to install the dimmer, concentrating on details that guarantee a safe installation.

The tools you'll need are inexpensive and will come in handy for all your electrical projects. You'll need a screwdriver, wire stripper, voltage tester and needle-nose pliers.

Double-check for hot wires in the box

Turn on the light and have a helper watch as you switch off the circuit breakers, or unscrew the fuses one at a time until the light goes out. Leave this circuit turned off while you work.

Use a noncontact voltage detector to double-check for voltage before removing the switch (Photo 1). These detectors are available at hardware stores and home centers for about $12. After you unscrew the switch and pull it away from the box, probe around inside the box with the detector to make sure there are no other hot wires from another circuit.

TOGGLE DIMMER

Make sure the box is large enough

Too many wires and devices stuffed into a box can cause dangerous overheating, short-circuiting and fires. The National Electrical Code specifies minimum box sizes to reduce this risk.

To figure the minimum box size required by the electrical code, add: 1 for each hot and neutral wire entering the box, 1 for all the ground wires combined, 1 for all the clamps combined, and 2 for each device (switch or receptacle) installed in the box. Multiply this figure by 2 for 14-gauge wire and 2.25 for 12-gauge wire to get the minimum box volume in cubic inches.

To help determine the gauge of the wire in your switch box, look at the amperage of the circuit breaker or fuse in the main electrical panel. Fifteen-amp circuits are usually wired with 14-gauge wire and 20-amp circuits require 12-gauge or heavier wire.

Compare the figure you get with the volume of your existing box. Plastic boxes have the volume stamped inside, usually on the back. Steel box capacities are listed in the electrical code. Figure A lists the volume of the most common steel boxes. If you have a steel box, measure it (Photo 2) and consult the chart to see if it's large enough. If your box is too small, replace it with a larger one. It's possible to replace a box without cutting away the wall, but it's a tricky job. Remove about a 16-in. square of drywall or plaster and patch it after the new large box is installed.

Test your ground before you connect it

New dimmers have either a green grounding wire or a green ground screw that you'll have to connect to a grounding source if one is available. Houses wired with plastic-sheathed cable almost always have bare copper ground wires that you'll connect to the dimmer. But test first using the procedure shown in Photo 3 to verify that the wire is connected to a ground.

Some wiring systems rely on metal conduit for the ground. If you have

ELECTRONIC DIMMER

Figure A
Common metal box sizes

Height/width/depth (inches)	Volume (cubic inches)
3 x 2 x 2-1/4	10.5
3 x 2 x 2-1/2	12.5
3 x 2 x 2-3/4	14.0

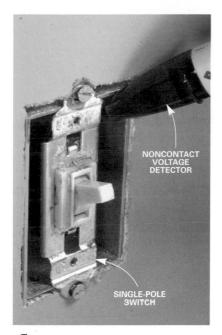

1 Turn off the power at the main circuit panel. Hold the tip of a non-contact voltage tester near each screw terminal to be sure the power is off. Then unscrew the switch and pull it from the box.

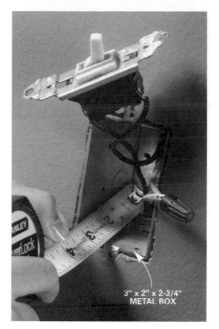

2 Measure the height, width and depth of metal boxes and refer to Figure A, p. 114, to determine the box volume. Plastic boxes have their volume stamped inside.

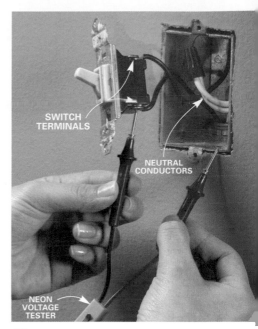

3 Test for a ground. Turn the power back on. Then place the leads of a voltage tester between each screw terminal and the metal box. If the tester lights, the box is grounded. Caution: Turn off the power again before proceeding.

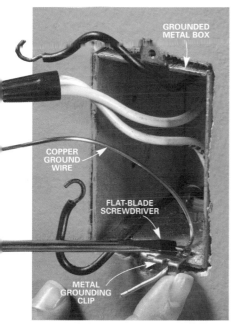

4 Press a grounding clip and 6-in. length of bare copper wire onto the metal box with a screwdriver. Cut away a little bit of drywall under the box to provide clearance for the clip.

5 Bend the ground wire back onto the clip and squeeze it down tight so it won't interfere with the dimmer switch.

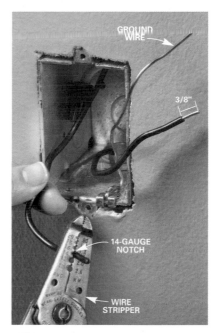

6 Clip off the bent end of each wire with the wire cutter. Strip 3/8 in. of insulation from the end of the wires.

one of these systems, Photo 3 shows how to test the metal box to verify that it's grounded. If it is, attach a short ground wire to the metal box with either a metal grounding clip as shown in Photos 4 and 5 or a green grounding screw screwed into the threaded hole in the back of the box. Then connect it to the dimmer.

If testing reveals your box isn't grounded, you can still install the dimmer, but you must use a plastic cover plate and make sure no bare metal parts are exposed.

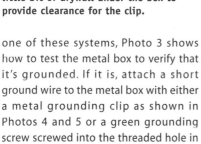

CAUTION:
If you have aluminum wiring, don't mess with it! Call in a licensed pro who's certified to work with it. This wiring is dull gray, not the dull orange that's characteristic of copper.

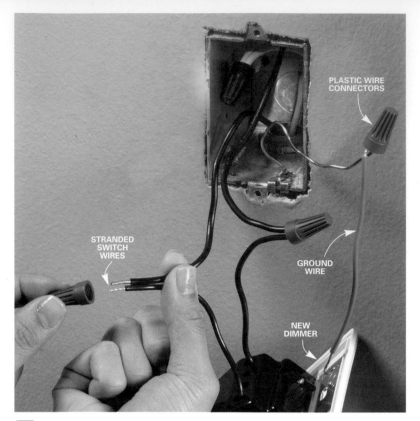

PLASTIC WIRE CONNECTORS

STRANDED SWITCH WIRES

GROUND WIRE

NEW DIMMER

NEW DIMMER SWITCH

SCREW TO BOX

7 Hold the wires together with the stranded wire protruding about 1/8 in. beyond the solid wire. Match the size of the wire connector you're using to the size and number of wires being connected. Check the manufacturer's specifications on the package to be sure. Twist a plastic wire connector clockwise onto the wires to connect them. Stop twisting when the connector is snug.

8 Fold the wires neatly into the box. Screw the dimmer to the box with the screws provided. Finish the job by installing the cover plate and turning on the power to test the new dimmer.

The easy part is installing the dimmer

Some dimmers, like the one shown here, have stranded wires attached. Photos 7 and 8 show how to install this type of dimmer. Others have screw terminals instead. For these, strip 3/4 in. of the insulated covering from the wires in the box and bend a loop in each with a needle-nose pliers. Place the loop clockwise around the screw terminals and close the loop around the screws with the needle-nose pliers. Then tighten the screws.

> **CAUTION:**
> Call an electrician if the original switch is connected to two white wires. This may indicate a dangerous switched neutral.

It doesn't matter if you reverse the two switch wires to a single-pole dimmer. But if you're replacing a three-way switch with a three-way dimmer, label the "common" wire (it'll be labeled on the old switch) when you remove the old switch so you can connect it to the "common" terminal on the dimmer.

In most cases, the two switch wires will be some color other than green or white, usually black. But one of the wires may be white if your house is wired with plastic-sheathed cable (like Romex). Put a wrap of black tape around the white conductor to label it as a hot wire.

> **✳ tip**
> If the circuit breaker is labeled "15 amp," the wires are probably 14 gauge, or 12 gauge for 20-amp circuit breakers.

Buying dimmers

If the switch you're replacing is the only switch controlling the light, buy a standard single-pole dimmer ($5 to $30). If the light can be switched on and off from two or more switches, buy a three-way dimmer switch. But you won't be able to dim the lights from every switch location unless you buy a set of special dimmers (about $70 per pair) with advanced electronics and install one at each switch location.

Most dimmers are designed to handle 600 watts. Add up the wattage of all the lightbulbs you'll be dimming. Then read the dimmer package to make sure it can handle the load. Heavy-duty 1,000- and 1,500-watt dimmers are also readily available. Read the package if you'll be installing dimmers side by side in the same electrical box because the wattage rating is reduced to compensate for extra heat buildup.

Finally, you have to use a special device, not a dimmer, to control the speed of ceiling fans and motors. Most fluorescent lightbulbs, unless they're labeled as "dimmable," can't be dimmed without altering the fixture.

79 Add a wireless switch

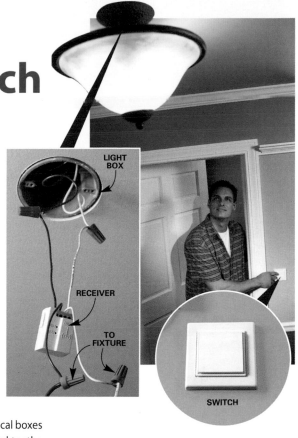

LIGHT BOX

RECEIVER

TO FIXTURE

SWITCH

Putting in a switch for an overhead fan, or wall outlet, or converting a two-way switch to a three-way switch can be a nightmare if you have to fish new wire through old walls and floors. With wallpapered walls and textured ceilings, it can be nearly impossible. Until recently, the only way around the problem was to buy a clunky battery-powered transmitter/receiver.

An entirely different type of switch is available: It converts the energy of a human finger pushing a switch into a radio signal strong enough to be picked up by a receiver in a light fixture or outlet up to 150 ft. away. Only 1/2 in. thick, the switch can be mounted on walls or woodwork or even glued to glass. The receivers come in two different types—one that's hidden inside the light box or outlet and one that plugs into the outlet.

Although the range is reduced by walls and ceilings, one switch can control an unlimited number of receivers, and one receiver can be programmed to respond to up to 30 switches.

To install the receiver, first turn off the power, then open the light or outlet box and wire the receiver between the power source and the light. Then push the "Learn" button on the receiver and click the switch so the receiver recognizes the signal. (Or buy a plug-in–type receiver.) Plastic electrical boxes work best—metal boxes can interfere with the signal. Install the receiver and try the switch a few times to make sure it's within range before you attach it to the wall.

The switches are available in either the square European style shown here or the traditional rocker style. The switch and receiver are available separately or as sets. Prices start at $60.

Buyer's Guide

Enocean wireless switches: (801) 225-2226.
www.adhocelectronics.com

Lightning transmitter/receiver: (888) 697-9482.
www.lightningswitch.com

80 Replace a **phone jack**

When your landline phone quits working or static develops on the line, your phone jack may need to be replaced. Here you'll learn how to handle the wiring and replace that phone jack for less than $5.

Remove the two screws on the jack faceplate and disconnect the old jack (Photo 1). Hold on to the wire when you remove the jack so it doesn't slide out the back of the box. If the ends of the wires are free of corrosion, you can reuse them, but if not, cut them back (leave enough wire to work with) and strip off 1/2 in. of sheathing. Photo 2 shows you how to reconnect those wires. If the wires from the wall and the jack are the same color combination, simply match them up. If they don't match, see the chart below. Before you mount the new jack to the wall, make sure the bare wires don't touch each other.

Std. cable	Corresponding colors in other cables	
Red	Blue	Blue/White dashes
Green	Blue/White	White/Blue dashes
Yellow	Orange	Orange/White dashes
Black	Orange/White	White/Orange dashes

1 Loosen the terminal screws on the back of the jack and disconnect the wiring.

OLD JACK

2 Pinch the wire sheathing against the back of the new jack with your thumb. Hold the tip of the bare wire with a needle-nose pliers, and wrap it clockwise around the terminal screw.

NEW JACK

81 Hang a quilt

One good way to display a quilt is to hang it on a wall. But don't just tack it up by the corners or it'll stretch out of shape. Instead, use this method for hanging quilts or other decorative textiles because it distributes the weight evenly for smooth hanging and minimal stress to the fabric. The hand stitching (Photo 1) used in this method doesn't damage the quilt because it only goes through the backing, and it's easy to remove when you no longer wish to display the quilt.

Measure the top edge of the quilt and purchase the same lengths of 1-1/2-in.-wide sew-on hook-and-loop fastener strip and 2-1/2-in.-wide cotton or synthetic webbing. Hook-and-loop strips are available at fabric stores, and the webbing at upholsterer's shops. You'll also need a length of 1-1/2-in.-wide pine or poplar, a staple gun and several 2-1/2-in. wood screws.

Photos 1 – 3 show how to prepare and hang the quilt. If the quilt pattern allows, it's best to rotate the quilt 180 degrees every month or so. This relieves stress on the fabric and helps prevent uneven fading. To be able to rotate the quilt, you'll have to sew another strip of hook-and-loop along the opposite edge.

It's usually not hard to hang things on drywall. Other types of walls present unique challenges. Plaster is harder than drywall and can crumble. But as long as you use professional picture hangers like the ones shown here (these have sharper nails and built-in angle guides), and use hangers a little larger than required, you'll usually be OK. In brick or stone, you can often drive a thin nail into the space between the mortar and the brick or stone. A good method for brick, stone or concrete walls is to drill a hole that's slightly smaller than the threaded part of a drywall screw. Use a masonry bit in a hammer drill and drill the hole at a slight downward angle. Then thread the screw into the hole, leaving about 1/4 in. sticking out for use as a hanger.

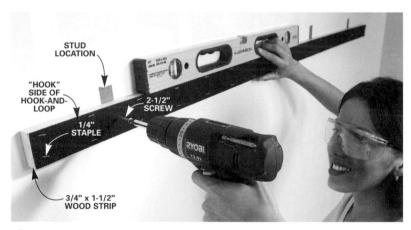

1 Sew the loop side of the hook-and-loop to the webbing. Then stitch the webbing to the back of the quilt using a herringbone stitch as shown.

2 Staple the hook side of the hook-and-loop to the wood strip. Determine the best position, and level the wood strip and screw it to the studs.

3 Hang the quilt by smoothing the hook-and-loop tape that's sewn on the back of the quilt along the tape stapled to the wood strip.

82 Add a **closet rod** and **shelf**

This project will save you hours of ironing and organizing. Now you can hang up your shirts and jackets as soon as they're out of the dryer—no more wrinkled shirts at the bottom of the basket. You'll also gain an out-of-the-way upper shelf to store all sorts of odds and ends.

Just go to your home center and get standard closet rod brackets, a closet rod and a precut 12-in.-deep melamine shelf (all for about $25). Also pick up some drywall anchors, or if you have concrete, some plastic anchors and a corresponding masonry bit. Follow the instructions in Photos 1 and 2. You can get these great-looking Lido Rail chrome brackets and rod at home centers or buy them online. One source is www.aubuchonhardware.com.

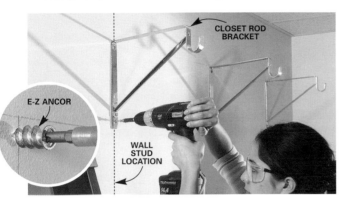

1 Draw a level line about 78 in. above the floor and locate the studs behind the drywall. Fasten at least two of your closet rod brackets into wall studs (4 ft. apart) and then center the middle bracket with two 2-in.-long screws into wall anchors (inset).

2 Fasten your 12-in.-deep Melamine shelf onto the tops of the brackets with 1/2-in. screws. Next, insert your closet rod, drill 1/8-in. holes into the rod, and secure it to the brackets with No. 6 x 1/2-in. sheet metal screws.

- -

83 Attach a **towel bar** to the laundry sink

Get those messy rags out of the sink and onto a towel bar so they can actually dry. Shop for an easy mounting towel bar (about $8) that you can shorten if you like. Pick one up at the hardware store that has easy mounting holes right on the face of the mounting plate and a removable bar. Cut the bar with a hacksaw so it will fit nicely on the side of the sink. While you're at the hardware store, buy stainless steel mounting bolts, washers and acorn nuts to mount the bar. Shown here are 7/8-in. No. 8-24 bolts.

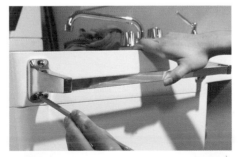

1 Mark the location of your towel bar on the thick rim near the top of the sink. You may need to shorten the bar first by pulling the bar from the ends and trimming it to about 16 in.

2 Drill clearance holes at your marks and fasten the towel bar ends to the sink with bolts, washers and acorn nuts.

84 Critter-proof your home

Shore up your lines of defense against unwanted guests. If mice, ants, spiders or other pests are getting into your home and claiming squatters' rights, it's time to evict them. Like any other guest, pests will only visit if you let them in. Once inside, they'll only stay if you make them comfortable. Here you'll learn three pest-fighting strategies. First, learn how to close the entryways that let critters in. Then you'll learn how to eliminate the moisture that sustains them and the clutter that provides a cozy habitat.

Find the passages that let pests in

If you can slide a pencil into a crack, it's large enough for a young mouse to squeeze through. Take your time and examine every square foot of your home. Here are the key areas to inspect:

- **Wall penetrations:** Search for gaps around anything that passes through your walls such as gas, plumbing and AC lines, phone and TV cables and exhaust vents.

- **Siding:** Gaps and holes in siding and around trim are usually obvious. But also look under the siding where it meets the foundation (Photo 1). Rot, foundation shifting and sloppy building practices can leave openings there.

- **Doors and windows:** Look for torn screens and worn-out weatherstripping that might provide an entryway for bugs. If

Eliminate pest entrances

Stop mice, squirrels, bats, beetles, ants and flies

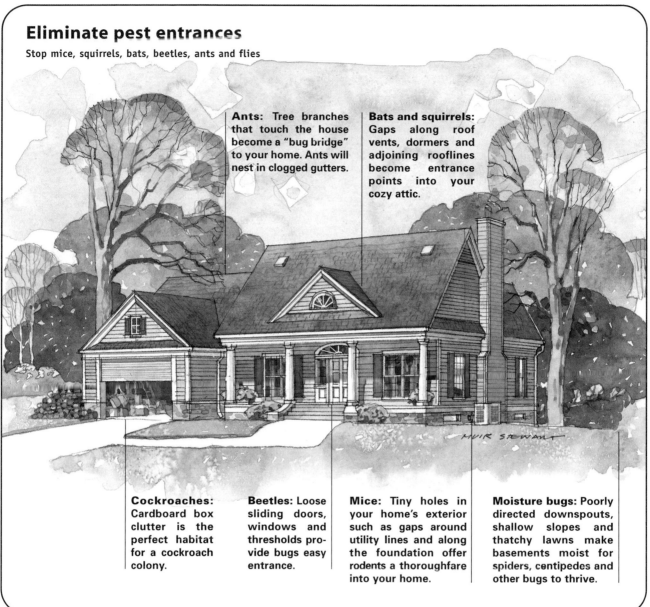

Ants: Tree branches that touch the house become a "bug bridge" to your home. Ants will nest in clogged gutters.

Bats and squirrels: Gaps along roof vents, dormers and adjoining rooflines become entrance points into your cozy attic.

Cockroaches: Cardboard box clutter is the perfect habitat for a cockroach colony.

Beetles: Loose sliding doors, windows and thresholds provide bugs easy entrance.

Mice: Tiny holes in your home's exterior such as gaps around utility lines and along the foundation offer rodents a thoroughfare into your home.

Moisture bugs: Poorly directed downspouts, shallow slopes and thatchy lawns make basements moist for spiders, centipedes and other bugs to thrive.

mice are a problem (and you have an attached garage), make sure the rubber gasket under your garage door seals tightly to the floor (replace the gasket if it doesn't seal).

- **Foundation:** Look for foundation settling cracks in masonry and make sure basement windows close and seal tightly (Photo 3). If there's a crawl space under your house, all the floors above the space are potential entry zones. If the crawl space is accessible, put on safety glasses, crawl inside and inspect it with a flashlight.

> **tip** Sometimes you can locate passageways from indoors. On a sunny day, light peeking into a dark basement, garage or attic reveals gaps and cracks. A heavy concentration of cobwebs indoors can also indicate an entry point.

- **Foliage or wood piles:** Anything touching your house can provide a freeway for bugs. Tree branches, for example, can spell trouble even high above ground level. Ants that feed on aphids in trees use branches as a bridge to your house. The solution is to trim back branches.

- **Dryer vents and exhaust fans:** Be sure that dampers open and close freely (Photo 3). Trouble starts when a sticking damper stays open and leaves a welcoming entrance for all sorts of critters, including birds and squirrels. Clean lint out of the vent. If the damper still won't close, replace the vent.

- **Soffits and roof:** Look for holes and gaps in soffits and fascia, especially where they run into adjoining rooflines (these are favorite entries for squirrels, bats and wasps).

- **Roof vents:** A missing or chewed-through screen on roof vents lets squirrels or bats into your attic.

1 Inspect the underside of your siding using a mirror. If you find a gap, mark the location with masking tape so you can seal it later.

2 Examine dryer vents to ensure the damper isn't stuck open or broken off completely. Also check that the seal between the vent and the wall is tight.

3 Seal doors, windows and basement sashes with adhesive-backed weatherstripping. Clean the surface first so the weatherstrip will adhere well.

4 Fill gaps between trim and siding with acrylic latex caulk. Keep a wet cloth handy to clean up any stray caulk. Smooth the bead with a wet finger.

■ **Chimney caps:** Add chimney caps if you don't already have them. They prevent birds and rodents from making the firebox of your fireplace their summer home.

■ **Gutters:** Debris-filled gutters are a favorite nesting spot for corn ants.

Plug up passages

Chances are you'll find several entry points in your walls, foundation or soffits. Fortunately, these gaps and cracks are easy to seal. For those smaller than 1/4 in. wide, acrylic latex caulk ($3 per tube) is a good filler because it's inexpensive, paintable and easy to apply (Photo 4). But acrylic caulk won't last long in wider gaps. For gaps and cracks 1/4 in. up to 1/2 in. wide, use polyurethane caulk ($5 per tube). Polyurethane is gooey and more difficult to use than acrylic caulk, but you can smooth and paint it for a neat-looking job. Keep a rag and mineral spirits handy to clean up accidents.

Expanding foam ($5 per can) is a fast, convenient filler for anything wider or for areas where appearance doesn't matter. It can fill gaps of any size but doesn't leave a smooth, neat-looking patch. Since rodents can gnaw right through foam, it's smart to stuff gaps with copper mesh before you add the foam (Photo 6). Conventional steel wool can eventually rust away. If you only have a few gaps to fill, buy a box of Chore Boy copper scrubbing pads for about $3 from a hardware store or online at www.walgreens.com. If you have holes galore, it may be

COPPER MESH

5 Pull nests from the soffit gaps and then fill these openings with expanding foam. After the foam hardens, cut off the excess with a utility knife.

6 Stuff in a generous amount of copper mesh with a screwdriver, leaving about half an inch of space for expanding foam sealant. Seal gaps with foam.

EXPANDING FOAM

COPPER MESH

7 Trim the foam flush using a utility knife after allowing the foam to harden overnight. To trim off a thicker section of foam, use an old steak knife.

cheaper to purchase a professional copper mesh product like CopperBlocker, which is available online at www.nixalite.com for $45 for a 100-ft. roll. For most cracks, "minimal expanding" foam is the easiest to use (standard foam expands too much, flows out of the crack and makes a mess). A little overflow is no problem, since you can slice off the excess (Photo 7). For large or hollow cavities, standard full-expansion foam is the best (Photo 5).

tip Before you sweep up mouse droppings, always spray them with a disinfectant spray such as Lysol. Mice can pass disease to humans through their waste.

Mousetrap technique

Snap-type mousetraps, when well placed, can be an effective way to rid your house of mice. Snap traps may seem cruel, but compared with a slow death from a glue trap or poisoned bait, they're a more humane way to exterminate mice. And because you toss the remains in the garbage, there are no dead mouse surprises to encounter later.

Common mistakes are poor placement of traps and using too few of them. Mice have poor vision and prefer to feel their way along walls. Place snap traps along walls in areas where you've seen the telltale brown pellets. For an average-size house, two dozen mousetraps would not be too many.

The best technique is to set two traps, parallel to the wall, with the triggers facing out. While mice can jump over one trap, they can't jump two. Favorite baits of professional exterminators are chocolate syrup and peanut butter.

Live traps are best used in pairs in the same manner as conventional mousetraps. Place them back-to-back with the open doors on each end.

Deprive bugs of moisture

Insects and other small pests need to draw life-sustaining moisture from their surroundings, so they avoid dry places and are attracted to moist ones. If your walls, foundation and the soil around your house already are dry, they'll be less attractive to insects, spiders and centipedes.

There's no way to keep everything perfectly dry, of course, but you can reduce moisture. Here are common moisture sources and ways to reduce them:

- **Downspouts and gutters:** Check that the downspouts are turned away from the house, and invest in a splash block or downspout extensions to disperse rainwater. Also watch for major leaks in your gutter system that may be pouring water onto or near your foundation.
- **Standing water:** If water is not absorbing into your lawn, your grass may have a buildup of thatch. The solution is to aerate your lawn to open up dense patches and admit water better.

- **Poor drainage:** Make sure that the soil is sloped away from the house at least 6 in. over 10 ft. This will reduce soil dampness near your foundation and keep your basement drier.
- **Mounded mulch:** Mulch and soil trap moisture and should be raked away from your windowsills and any other wood (Photo 1).
- **Heavy vegetation:** Plants growing against the house will keep siding damp. Trim back bushes and trees.
- **Plumbing leaks:** Fix leaks such as a dripping hose bib. If your home is above a crawl space, look for leaks from any exposed plumbing under the house.

Moisture problems can come from inside the home too. A leaky sink trap, for example, can create a moist bug oasis under your kitchen cabinets. A poor seal around a bathtub can allow water into the surrounding floor and walls. Damp basements are a favorite home for spiders, centipedes, millipedes, silverfish and sowbugs.

1 Rake moisture-wicking soil and mulch away from the window frames and low wood. Turn your mulch periodically to help keep dampness down, and keep bushes trimmed back.

2 If you suspect an area is damp, use a screwdriver to probe the wood to determine if it's soft and moist. Eliminate the moisture source and replace rotten wood.

Spider solution

You can virtually eliminate spiders in your basement by using a dehumidifier to maintain a 40 percent humidity level and vigilantly sweeping down cobwebs whenever they appear. Keep the basement windowsills brushed clean too. In a matter of weeks, the spider population will die down significantly.

Eliminate clutter

If pests are the enemy, then clutter is the battlefield. Any pests you can name love untidiness for a couple of reasons: to hide their initial infestation and provide privacy and shelter for reproduction.

The best way to eliminate pest homes is to store items properly. Garages often harbor many clutter zones and are easily accessible to critters. Add to that the seductive smells of pet chow and your garage will look pretty darn cozy to pests looking for a home. Birdseed and pet food need to be stored in containers that mice and other rodents can't get into (Photo 1). Avoid keeping old cardboard boxes in your garage, but if you must, make sure they are broken down neatly, stored off the floor and inspected regularly.

Neatness deters pests indoors, too. Keep cardboard boxes and even plastic bins off the floor and on a wire rack or shelf. Be especially rigorous on concrete floors. Moisture forms between the concrete floor and the box bottom (silverfish especially love damp spaces under boxes). Another reason to use storage racks is for easier pest inspections. With boxes off the floor, you can quickly spot mouse droppings and other evidence of unwanted critters (Photo 2).

The cabinet under the kitchen sink is a potential pest nirvana with trash, moisture, clutter and dark hiding places. Infestations can be hard to spot under all the sponges, rubber gloves and paper bags. To get on track, take everything out of the cabinet and stick self-adhesive vinyl tile squares to the cabinet floor. These tiles are cheap (about $1 per 12 x 12-in. tile at home centers) and easy to wipe clean. Next put all your cleaning supplies in a tote so you can easily remove them to inspect and clean (Photo 3). While you're under there, be sure to check for plumbing leaks.

1 Store pet food in a lidded metal trash can, as mice cannot climb the slick, vertical sides of the can. Sealed plastic containers are also a good option.

2 Store items off the floor on wire rack shelving to prevent moisture from collecting underneath. Look for mouse droppings and other evidence of infestation with a flashlight and mirror.

3 Tidy up under the kitchen sink. Store items in a caddy so you can easily clear out the cabinet for cleaning and inspection. Self-adhesive tiles provide an easy-to-clean surface.

SELF-ADHESIVE VINYL TILES

Stop **water hammer**

If your plumbing bangs and clangs like a truckload of scrap metal, you've got "water hammer." Water develops momentum as it flows fast through pipes. When a valve closes quickly and stops the flow, that momentum shakes and pounds pipes. Water hammer arresters cure this condition with a cushion of air that absorbs the momentum. Before you install arresters, determine which faucets or valves in your house cause the noise. Washing machines and dishwashers are prime suspects because their automatic valves close fast. Arresters for washing machines have screw-on connections, making them as easy to attach as a garden hose. Other arresters connect directly to 1/2-in. pipe, often under sinks. You usually have to cut pipes and add tees to install them. Check the packaging for installation details. Arresters cost about $10 each at home centers and hardware stores.

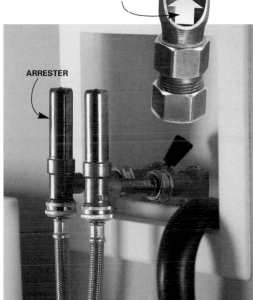

AIR CHAMBER

SLIDING PISTON

WATER MOMENTUM

ARRESTER

86 Paint with an airless sprayer

An airless sprayer simplifies painting in two ways: First, if you want to speed up a job that requires several gallons of paint, you can apply it twice as fast as with a roller or brush. And second, if you want a glass-smooth finish on woodwork or doors, the airless sprayer can lay the paint on flawlessly.

An airless sprayer works by pumping paint at a very high pressure, up to 3,000 psi, through a hose and out a tiny hole in the spray gun tip. The tip is designed to break up the paint evenly into a fan-shaped spray pattern of tiny droplets. Using different tips, you can spray thin liquids like stain, lacquer and varnish or thicker liquids like latex house paint. With a little practice, you can use an airless sprayer to apply a perfectly smooth finish on doors, cabinets and woodwork. And since an airless sprayer pumps paint directly from a can or 5-gallon bucket, you can apply a lot of material in a short time.

This makes an airless sprayer well suited for large paint jobs, like priming bare drywall in a new house or painting a 300-ft.-long fence.

But before you get too excited about the benefits of spray painting, there are a few drawbacks. First, the fine particles of paint don't all stick to the surface. A large percentage of the paint ends up in the air, where it can drift and settle onto everything in sight. This means you'll be wasting 20 to 40 percent of the finish, depending on the application. You'll also have to mask off and cover everything you want to keep paint free. Outdoor painting is especially risky. Overspray can end up on your shrubs or roof, or drift with the wind onto your neighbor's car.

The other downside is the extra time it takes to flush the paint from the pump and hose and clean up the spray gun. If you're using your own sprayer, rather than a rental unit, you'll also have to clean the filters and install special storage fluid. And if you're spraying oil-based products, you'll have to store or recycle a gallon or two of used solvents left over from the cleaning process. But despite these disadvantages, an airless sprayer can save you a lot of time on big paint jobs and allow you to get a finish that's nearly impossible to get with a brush.

Rent or buy?

Airless sprayers start at about $200. Spending more doesn't necessarily get you more features, but it does get you a bigger, better motor and pump, which will deliver longer life and trouble-free operation. Owning a sprayer allows you to spray whenever you want and to ensure that the sprayer is clean and well maintained.

Renting is a good option if you don't expect to use the sprayer very often and want to avoid the extra maintenance. You can rent an airless sprayer for about $75 per day. Make sure the

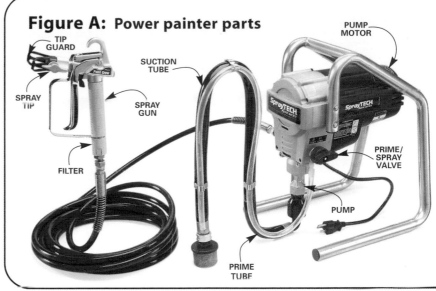

Figure A: Power painter parts

hose and pump are clean and that the filters have been cleaned or replaced. Ask for help in choosing the right spray tip for the job. Some rental stores won't allow you to spray oil-based products like lacquer, oil stain or oil-based paint, so be sure to ask.

Setting up the sprayer

Whether you rent or buy an airless sprayer, there are a few key setup points. All sprayers have a screen at the intake point. Make sure it's clean. Most sprayers also have a removable filter near the pump and another one in the handle of the gun. Check both to make sure they're clean, and plan to strain your paint through a mesh filter bag to remove lumps so they won't clog the filters.

Prime the pump

Before you can start spraying, you have to prime the pump. Photos 1 and 2 show how. You may have to repeat this process if the paint in the bucket runs out while you're spraying.

Prime the pump

1 Place the smaller prime tube in a waste pail and the suction tube in the bucket of strained paint. Turn the prime/spray valve to "prime." Switch on the pump. Turn the pressure valve up until the pump starts. When the paint starts flowing from the prime tube, move it into the paint bucket.

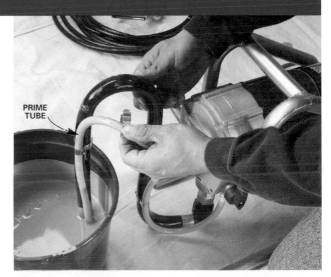

2 Clip the prime tube to the suction tube. Let the pump run for about 30 seconds or until no more air bubbles come out of the tube.

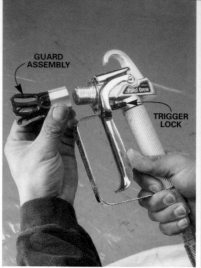

SPRAY GUN (GUARD AND TIP REMOVED)

GUARD ASSEMBLY

TRIGGER LOCK

SPRAY TIP

3 Hold the gun (guard and spray tip removed) over the waste bucket and pull the trigger. Switch the valve to the "spray" setting. Let go of the trigger when paint is flowing in a steady stream from the gun. Lock the trigger and follow the "Pressure Relief Steps" (see below, right).

4 Screw the guard assembly loosely onto the gun and align the guard at a 90-degree angle to your desired spray pattern. Insert the spray tip until the tab is engaged. Rotate the tip to face the arrow forward. Snug the guard assembly hand-tight.

Choose the right tip

Spray tips slide into a hole in the front of the gun. They're labeled with a three-digit number like 309 or 517 (these may be the last three digits of a longer model number). Doubling the first digit tells you the spray fan width with the gun held 12 in. from the surface. A 415 tip, for example, would have an 8-in.-wide fan, while a 515 would have a 10-in. fan pattern.

The next two digits indicate the size of the hole in thousandths of an inch. Choose a smaller diameter hole (.009 to .013) for thin liquids like stain or varnish and a larger hole (.015 or .017) for thicker liquids like latex paint.

A 411 tip would work well for spraying varnish on woodwork, while a 517 is a good size for spraying large surfaces with latex paint.

SPRAY TIP

Adjust the pressure

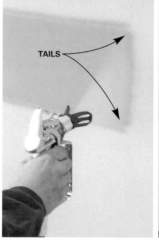

TAILS

EVEN PATTERN

5 Turn on the pump and move the prime/spray lever to the "spray" position. Spray a strip of paint across a piece of cardboard to check the spray pattern. If the spray pattern has tails (left), the pressure is set too low. Turn up the pressure until the paint is evenly distributed across the fan pattern (right).

If paint won't come out of the prime tube, the problem may be a clogged screen or filter, or a stuck ball-check valve in the pump assembly. If the sprayer you're using doesn't have a push-button on the pump to free the stuck ball, try to dislodge it by gently tapping the lowest end of the pump with a hammer. Otherwise follow the suggested troubleshooting procedure in your manual or call the rental store for help.

Fill the hose and set up the gun

Once the pump is primed, you're ready to fill the hose with paint (Photo 3). Then lock the trigger and relieve the pressure before installing the tip guard assembly and inserting the tip (Photo 4).

Pressure relief steps

1. Turn off the power switch.
2. Turn the spray/prime valve to prime.
3. Aim the gun against the side of the waste pail and pull the trigger to release the pressure.
4. Engage the trigger lock.

Adjust the pressure

Too little pressure will result in an uneven spray pattern. And too much pressure causes excessive overspray and premature tip wear. Photo 5 shows how to dial in just the right amount. If you're still getting "tails" or an uneven spray pattern even at maximum

Airless sprayer safety

If you rent a sprayer, ask for a list of precautions. Here are the most important ones:

- Keep the trigger locked and follow the pressure relief procedure when you stop spraying, before cleaning, and before servicing the sprayer or installing tips. Never put your hand in front of the sprayer tip unless the unit is off and depressurized. The high-pressure spray can inject paint under your skin, causing a serious poisoning hazard. If you do puncture your skin with the spray, get to a doctor immediately.
- Wear safety glasses and an approved respirator when you're spraying.
- Work in a well-ventilated area.

CAUTION: When you're spraying flammable oil-based products, follow all grounding precautions to prevent sparks. Read your manual or ask the rental store for instructions on grounding the gun and metal pail.

Cleaning the tip

REVERSED TIP DIRECTION

If paint stops flowing or sputters from the gun, the tip may be clogged. Twist the tip 180 degrees. Point the gun at a scrap of paper and squeeze the trigger to clear the clog. Rotate the tip 180 degrees to point it forward again and spray a test strip onto the scrap.

Spraying techniques

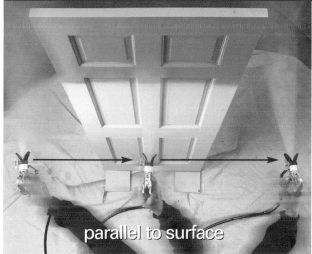

parallel to surface

50 PERCENT OVERLAP

RIGHT ANGLE TO SURFACE

6 Squeeze the trigger before you reach the edge of the door. Move the sprayer quickly across the door, keeping it parallel to the surface. Release the trigger when the sprayer is past the opposite edge of the door.

7 Overlap about half of the previously painted strip when you make the next pass with the sprayer. Keep the gun perpendicular to the surface.

pressure, try using a tip with a smaller hole. If the spray pattern is round rather than narrow, the tip is worn and should be replaced.

Spraying technique

See Photos 6 and 7 for the correct spray techniques, plus:

- Plan your spraying sequence before you start. On doors, for example, spray the edges first. Then spray top to bottom. Then spray at right angles side to side.
- Squeeze the trigger while the gun is off to the side, and then move it onto the work (Photo 6).
- Move the gun parallel to the surface, not in an arc.
- Keep the gun perpendicular to the surface, not tilted (Photo 7).

- Move fast to prevent runs. Several thin coats are better than one thick one.
- Overlap your strokes about 30 to 50 percent.

Troubleshooting

Most spray problems are a result of clogged filters, a clogged tip, or a pump that's either leaking at the packing or has stuck ball-check valves. Careful cleaning and proper maintenance will prevent most of these troubles.

Other problems, such as runs and uneven coverage, are caused by using the wrong tip size or by a lack of spraying experience. As with most tasks, practice is the key to success.

87 **Stop drafts** around windows and doors

If your windows or doors are a source of chilly drafts all winter long, the problem could be worn-out seals, weatherstripping or thresholds. Then again, sloppy installation might be to blame. When cold weather arrives, hold the back of your hand near the edges of windows or doors to track down the source of leaks. If you feel cold air flowing out from behind the trim, chances are the spaces around the window and doorjambs weren't properly sealed.

You have to pull off the interior trim, seal around the jambs and then reinstall the trim. But if your doors and windows are otherwise fairly airtight, the payoff can be big too. Stopping drafts not only makes your home more comfortable but also cuts energy bills (air leaks are a major source of heat loss in most homes).

First investigate further: Remove one piece of trim from a window or a door. To prevent chipping or tearing paint, cut through the paint first (Photo 1).

Slip a stiff putty knife under the trim and lift it enough to insert a flat pry bar. Don't simply force up one end of the piece. Instead, work along the length of the piece, moving your pry bar and lifting the trim off gradually (Photo 2). At mitered corners, watch for nails driven through the joint. To prevent these nails from splitting mitered ends, pry up both mitered pieces together. Then pull them apart. When you're removing nails from the trim, pull them through the back side to avoid damaging the face of the trim (Photo 3).

With one piece removed, examine the space between the jamb and the wall framing. If the drywall covers the space, trim it back with a utility knife. If you see only a few loose wads of fiberglass insulation or no insulation at all between the jamb and framing, it's likely that all your windows and doors are poorly sealed.

To seal the gap, remove the remaining trim and inject foam sealant (Photo 4). Some sealants will push jambs inward as they expand, so be sure to use one that's intended for windows and doors (check the label). DAP Tex Plus ($7) works great because it's easy to clean up with a damp rag. Most expanding foams are nearly impossible to clean up before they harden.

Let the foam harden and trim off any excess foam with a knife before you reinstall the trim. Position each piece exactly as it was originally and tack each one up with only two nails (Photo 5). When all the pieces are in place, check their fit. With only a couple of nails in each piece, you can make small adjustments by holding a block against the trim and tapping it with a hammer. Then add more nails.

If your trim has a clear finish, fill the nail holes with a matching colored filler such as Color Putty or DAP Finishing Putty ($3). With painted trim, it's best to fill the holes with spackle ($3) and repaint.

CAUTION:
Lead paint chips are hazardous. If your home was built before 1978, call your local health department for information on testing and handling lead paint safely.

1 Slice through paint where the trim meets the wall and jamb. Put a new blade in your utility knife and make several passes over heavy paint buildup.

2 Pry away the trim gently with a flat pry bar. Protect walls with a shim or a scrap of wood as you gradually work the trim away from the wall.

SHIM   FLAT PRY BAR

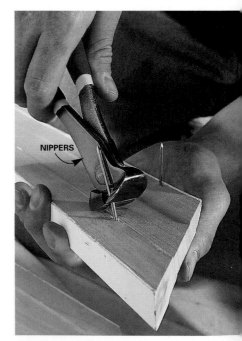

NIPPERS

3 Pull nails out through the back side of trim with a nippers or a pliers. Also write the location of each piece of trim on the back side.

88 Adjust a **storm door**

If your storm door slams shut or won't close hard enough to latch, try a few simple adjustments to make it close just right.

First, change the mounting position of the closer's connecting pin (Photo 1). To remove the pin, you have to first lock the door open with the hold-open washer to release the tension on the pin. But there's a good chance that your hold-open washer won't work. In that case, open the door and snap a locking pliers (such as a Vise-Grip pliers) onto the closer shaft to hold the door open. To repair the washer, slip it off the shaft, put it in a vise and make a sharper bend in it using a hammer. Or you can take the entire closer to a home center or hardware store and find a similar replacement for about $10. Some closers mount a little differently from the one shown. For example, you may find that the door bracket, rather than the closer, has two holes for pins.

If moving the pin makes matters worse, return it to its original position and try the adjustment screw (Photo 2). Turn it clockwise for a softer close, counterclockwise for harder. If your door has two closers, treat them exactly alike. Adjust both screws equally and make sure their pins are in the same position.

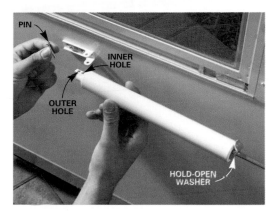

1 Lock the door open and remove the pin. Connect the closer at the inner hole to make the door close harder. For a softer close, use the outer hole.

2 Turn the adjustment screw to make the door close harder or softer. Make a quarter turn, test the door and continue making quarter turns until the door closes just right.

4 Pull any pieces of insulation from between the jamb and the wall framing. Seal the gap around the jamb with foam sealant.

5 Tack each section of trim exactly in its original position with a couple of nails. Ridges in the wall paint can help you align each piece perfectly. Make sure the parts fit together tightly at the corners before you add more nails.

89 Change your transmission fluid

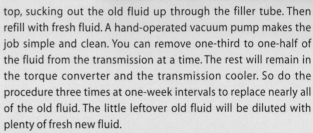

You should change your automatic transmission fluid according to the manufacturer's recommendation—whether that's 30,000 or 100,000 miles. This maintenance task will add tens of thousands of miles—which could be years of service—to a transmission's life expectancy and prevent repairs costing thousands down the road.

New fluid is bright red.

This transmission fluid has been working for 60,000 miles. It turns brown as it degrades—time to change.

A transmission flush-and-fill from a shop will cost you $149 to $199. But you can do it yourself and save about $100. Draining the old fluid has always been a messy, ugly job. That's because it has meant lying under the car, "dropping" the pan, and then getting drenched in fluid. But here's a new way to change your fluid without going under the car and without spilling a drop. The procedure takes less than 30 minutes.

The trick is to work from the top, sucking out the old fluid up through the filler tube. Then refill with fresh fluid. A hand-operated vacuum pump makes the job simple and clean. You can remove one-third to one-half of the fluid from the transmission at a time. The rest will remain in the torque converter and the transmission cooler. So do the procedure three times at one-week intervals to replace nearly all of the old fluid. The little leftover old fluid will be diluted with plenty of fresh new fluid.

Some manufacturers recommend replacing the filter every time you change the transmission fluid. Go with what your dealership recommends. Note: But if your transmission pan is leaking, you should either "drop" the pan and replace the gasket, or take it in for service.

1 Remove the dipstick and insert the vacuum tube until you feel it "bottom out" on the bottom of the transmission pan.

2 Close the latch on the vinyl hose and pump up the vacuum tank with 30 to 50 strokes of the plunger.

3 Release the latch on the hose and wait while the vacuum draws the old fluid out.

4 Read on the tank the amount of fluid you withdrew and refill the transmission with that amount of new fluid.

LIQUIVAC FLUID PUMP, $33

This pump is the key to saving you time and money when you change your transmission fluid. Buy it on Amazon.com from seller Nobel Direct.

Buy the right stuff

Carmakers have made major improvements to transmission fluids in the past two years. Contact the dealership parts department to see if your car requires a newer fluid. Then call auto parts stores until you find one that stocks it. If you strike out, bite the bullet and buy it from the dealer (dealers usually charge more than auto parts stores).

90 Clean your **MAF sensor**

A mass air flow (MAF) sensor monitors the temperature and weight of air entering your engine.

The sensor works by heating a delicate platinum wire or plate and measuring the current required to keep it at a constant temperature while air blows past it. Over time, dust and oil particles stick to the hot wire/plate and bake on. Eventually, those baked-on particles cause starting, idling, acceleration problems, and poor gas mileage.

Carmakers recommend that you replace the MAF sensor ($300) at that point. But if you clean your car's MAF sensor regularly, you can avoid that $300 repair and keep your engine running at top efficiency. The cleaner only costs $7! Clean the MAF sensor every time you change your air filter. Here's how:

Before going to the store, pull off the air duct between the air filter box and the throttle body to see how the MAF sensor is anchored. If you see Torx screws, buy a Torx tool and a can of CRC Mass Air Flow Sensor Cleaner. *Don't use any other cleaners; they can ruin the MAF.* Everything you need is available at CarQuest, Advance and O'Reilly auto parts stores.

Locate the MAF sensor in the air duct between the air filter box and the throttle body. Before you remove the sensor, use a digital camera to record the sensor setup and connections for

PLATINUM WIRE

MAF SENSOR

AIR DUCT

ELECTRICAL CONNECTOR

reference later. Carefully remove the sensor from the air duct and disconnect the electrical connector.

Spray 10 to 15 spurts of the cleaner onto the wire or plate. Don't scrub the parts; you may break the wire or damage the plate. Allow the MAF sensor to dry completely before reinstalling it in the air duct.

91 Repair **weather stripping**

During cold weather, water can freeze around the door's weather strip, locking you out of your car. If you pull hard to break the ice, the weather strip can tear right off the door. Here's how to fix the weather strip and prevent it from tearing again.

Buy a tube of weather-strip adhesive, a can of nonflammable spray brake cleaner and a can of spray silicone (all are available at any auto parts store). Then pull the weather strip away from the door and clean it and the metal surface with the brake cleaner. Let that dry completely, then squeeze a bead of the adhesive onto the weather strip and the door and let that dry. Then apply a second coat to both surfaces and press the weather strip into place. Clean up any adhesive messes with the brake cleaner.

Hold the weather strip in place with masking tape until the adhesive dries (about 45 minutes). Then remove the tape and spray silicone on the weather strip on the other doors and trunk lid.

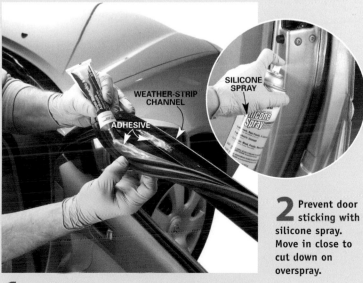

WEATHER-STRIP CHANNEL

ADHESIVE

SILICONE SPRAY

2 Prevent door sticking with silicone spray. Move in close to cut down on overspray.

1 Apply adhesive to the back of the weather strip and the channel.

92 Replace **spark plugs** yourself

You already know that spark plugs wear out. Over time, the gap grows to the point where the spark can no longer make the jump. That's when you get misfires, poor gas mileage, lousy acceleration and, ultimately, the dreaded "Check Engine" light.

To keep vehicles running at peak performance for longer service intervals, many car manufacturers install extended-life spark plugs. Because their electrodes are coated with precious metals that have higher melting points, these plugs can sometimes maintain a precise gap for up to 100,000 miles. But even with higher melting points, metals like yttrium (2,779° F), platinum (3,222° F) and iridium (4,429° F) can't stave off erosion forever.

Replacing spark plugs

Unlike manufacturers' guidelines for oil changes, which are overly cautious, the recommendations for spark plug replacement intervals tend to be overly optimistic. For example, if you've already got 80,000 miles on a set of 100,000-mile plugs, they're 80 percent worn and beginning to take a toll on engine performance and gas mileage. Worse yet, after that many miles, spark plugs have a tendency to seize in the cylinder head. Removing a seized plug can be a costly job, especially if the threads in the cylinder head are damaged in the process. When you consider the gas mileage falloff and the possibility of seized plugs, early replacement makes sense.

Do it yourself?

The answer depends on the type of engine in your vehicle. Some V-6 models have very difficult spark-plug replacement procedures that require removing portions of the intake manifold. If you're not comfortable with that level of disassembly, you should take your vehicle to a pro. But if you have an engine with easy access to the rear bank, then you can probably do the job yourself. Just be sure you gap the spark plugs properly and use a torque wrench.

The tools shown are available at www.tooldiscounter.com and CarQuest auto stores.

1 Wait for the engine to cool before removing plugs. Using a spark plug wire puller, grasp the boot as far down on the plug as possible, twist and pull straight out.

SWIVEL SOCKET

2 Blow debris away from the spark plug recess before removing the spark plug. Using the swivel spark plug socket and an extension, unscrew the spark plug.

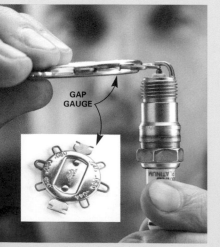

GAP GAUGE

3 Gap all plugs before installation using the manufacturer's specs. Slide a gap gauge between the center and the side electrodes and adjust the electrode to achieve a slight drag on the gauge. Place a small dab of antiseize compound on the plug threads and hand-thread the plug into the cylinder head.

TORQUE WRENCH

4 Proper spark plug torque is *critical* in today's engines. *Always* use a torque wrench and the manufacturer's torque specifications! Insufficient torque can result in a plug blowing right out of the cylinder head, taking the threads with it. Too much torque distorts the plug. If you used anti-seize compound on the plug threads, reduce torque by 10 percent.

93 Treat your windshield glass

Glass treatment products can improve your view through your windshield in rainy weather by as much as 34 percent. The improved vision can increase your response rate by up to 25 percent. That could mean the difference between avoiding an accident or being part of one.

Most glass treatments coat your windshield with a water-repellent silicone film. The coating makes water bead up so the wiper blade can more easily remove it. The coating also makes it easier to wipe off ice and bugs.

A new glass treatment called Aquapel chemically bonds with the glass and lasts for six months. Many auto parts stores sell Aquapel for $10.

Application of Aquapel is simple. Make sure the temperature is at least 50 degrees F. Clean the windshield and allow the glass to dry. Then wipe Aquapel onto the glass and wipe it off. Then wipe on a second coat, wipe it off and you're done.

Treated | Untreated

Photo courtesy of PPG Industries

Squeeze the wings on the Aquapel applicator to start the flow of the fluid. Apply to the windshield. Wipe off. Repeat.

94 Touch up scratches

Sometimes the small brushes that come with vehicle touch-up paint slop the paint on and make the repair look worse than the scratch. Try using a toothpick: The tip of the toothpick fills the scratch with just the right amount of paint.

95 Lube your door locks

You probably don't think much about your door locks until the key breaks off in the cylinder. Keep these delicate mechanisms moving freely with a blast of dry graphite powder. You may need to push the dust protector flap back slightly with a small metal nail file to get at the lock. A quick pump of the tube will dispense enough graphite. Move the lock cylinder with your key several times to work the graphite into the mechanism. Do this to your trunk lock as well.

96 Insulate rim joists, cut heat loss and save money

In just a couple of hours, you can seal and insulate your rim joists, which are a major source of heat loss in many homes. Properly insulating and air-sealing rim joists takes patience, so some builders simply stuff in some fiberglass and walk away.

The materials will cost about $1 per foot of rim joist. Call your local building inspections department before you begin this project. The inspector may require you to cover the new insulation with drywall (as a fire block) or leave some areas uncovered to allow for termite inspections. You can insulate second-floor rim joists following the same steps shown here if you happen to tear out a ceiling during remodeling.

Rigid foam is the best insulation for rim joists. Shown here is 2-in.-thick (R-10) "extruded polystyrene" ($20 per 4 x 8-ft. sheet). Don't use "expanded polystyrene," which is a less effective air and moisture barrier.

Cut the foam into 8-ft.-long strips 1/8 in. less than the height of the rim joist. A table saw is the fastest way to "rip" these strips, but you can also use a circular saw. Then cut the strips to length to fit between the joists, again cutting them 1/8 in. short (Photo 1). A heavy-duty box cutter ($6) is the best knife for making short cuts and trimming foam; the long blade slices cleanly through the foam (a utility knife blade is too short). Use long sections of foam to cover the rim joists that are parallel to the floor joists (Photo 2). Don't worry about cutting the foam for a tight fit around pipes, cables or other obstructions; you can seal large gaps with expanding foam sealant later.

FLOOR JOIST FOAM INSULATION

1 Cut rigid foam insulation into strips with a table saw or a circular saw. Cut the strips to fit between floor joists using a box cutter.

BOX CUTTER

CAULK

RIM JOIST

EXPANDING FOAM

2 Run a bead of acrylic caulk around each section of foam to form an airtight barrier. Fill gaps larger than 1/4 in. with expanding foam sealant.

It's important to create an airtight seal around each section of foam using caulk or expanding foam (Photo 2). Otherwise, moist inside air could condense on the cold rim joist. The resulting dampness can lead to mold and rot. If you have a solid concrete foundation, also run a bead of caulk where the sill plate meets the concrete. If you have a concrete block foundation, also seal the openings on top with expanding foam. Stuff a wad of fiberglass insulation into each opening to support the foam as it hardens (see Figure A, below).

97 Apply heat-reducing window film

A heat-control window film will help keep a room cooler, and you can install it yourself. These films reflect the sun's heat and ultraviolet rays, and reduce glare without obscuring the view (see photo). The more direct sunlight coming through the window, the more the film will help (and it may lower your air-conditioning bills!).

Applying the film takes approximately 30 minutes per window. The film should last about 10 years. Prices vary with film size. A 3-ft. x 15-ft. piece of film (which can cover two to three windows) costs $30. The film is sold at home centers and hardware stores. Gila is one company that makes heat-control film (800-528-4481, www.gilafilms.com).

Different types of film are available, so get the one designed for heat control. The film can be applied to any window, including double-pane low-E windows, although they already reduce radiant heat loss and gain.

One drawback is that the film may void the manufacturer's warranty for the seal on double-pane windows, although the film shouldn't affect the seal. If the window warranty has already expired or reducing excessive heat is more important to you than possibly jeopardizing a warranty, then apply the film.

Window film can be installed in about 30 minutes. The hazy appearance will disappear after 10 days.

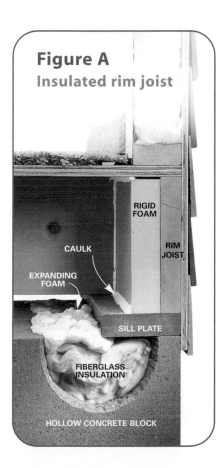

Figure A
Insulated rim joist

RIGID FOAM

RIM JOIST

CAULK

EXPANDING FOAM

SILL PLATE

FIBERGLASS INSULATION

HOLLOW CONCRETE BLOCK

FILM   NO FILM

Heat-control film is composed of treated micro-thin layers of film that block ultraviolet rays and reduce the summer heat that comes through the window.

98 Seal **air leaks**

Keep a can of expanding foam and a caulk gun handy and plug obvious electrical cable holes and fixture boxes in your attic. Make sure you get to the plumbing vent, because the gap around it is usually large (Photo 1). Also look for the 2x4 top plates (framing) of interior walls and follow them, keeping a sharp eye out for electrical cable holes and dirty insulation, which would indicate a gap or long crack between drywall and a wood plate. Seal these with latex caulk.

Work carefully with expanding foam because it's super

sticky and almost impossible to get off your clothes and skin. Wear disposable gloves when working with it.

Seal the access hatch with self-sticking foam weatherstrip (Photo 3). You may have to add new wood stops to provide a better surface for the weatherstrip and enough room for hook-and-eye fasteners (Photo 4). Position the screw eyes so that you slightly compress the weatherstrip when you latch the hatch. Use a similar procedure if you have a hinged door that leads to the attic.

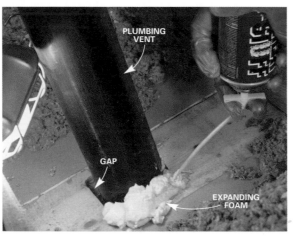

1 Stuff fiberglass batt insulation into the space around the plumbing vent pipe as a backer for the expanding foam. Then follow the directions on the can to fill the space around the pipe.

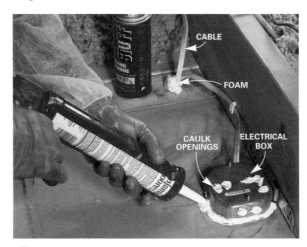

2 Fill wiring and plumbing holes with expanding foam. Caulk around electrical junction boxes and plug holes in the box with caulk.

3 Weatherstrip the attic access hatch or door. Cut 1x3 stops and nail them on with 6d finish nails. Apply self-adhesive foam weatherstrip to the top edge of the stop.

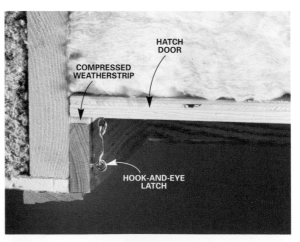

4 Attach hook-and-eye fasteners to the door and stops. Position the eyes so that the weatherstrip is compressed when you latch the hooks.

99 Protect outdoor furniture

If you'd like to preserve the natural wood appearance of your wood entry door or your outdoor furniture, take a lesson from boat builders. Boat builders and restorers use multiple coats of epoxy and spar varnish to protect wood—instead of spar varnish alone—because the combination is much stronger than either finish is separately. Epoxy creates a tough, flexible moisture barrier; spar varnish adds depth and UV protection, which keeps the epoxy from yellowing and eventually disintegrating.

The epoxy, a special type for clear-coating wood, is sold at woodworking suppliers, hobby shops and marine supply stores (see Buyer's Guide). It's expensive—the 2 quarts used here cost $70—but when fully cured, the finish is very tough and will last for years.

To begin, sand and clean the wood, then stain it if desired. Mix the resin and hardener thoroughly in a disposable container. A batch will start to harden in about 30 minutes, faster if it's hot out, so just mix a small quantity the first time to see how far you get. Apply the epoxy with an inexpensive natural-bristle brush (Photo 1). You'll need a new brush for each coat. When the epoxy in the container starts to stiffen and feel warm, discard the container and the brush and mix a new batch.

tip **Two-part epoxy**
Mix the resin and hardener thoroughly in a clean, disposable container, in the proportions specified by the manufacturer.

Allow the epoxy finish to harden overnight, then sand thoroughly and apply another coat. The manufacturer recommends three coats.

Sand the final coat of epoxy after it has cured for at least 24 hours (Photo 2), then vacuum the surface and wipe it with a damp rag. Topcoat the epoxy with a minimum of three coats of exterior spar varnish (Photo 3). Add coats of varnish every few years to keep the finish looking fresh.

Buyer's Guide

You can find epoxy for clear-coating wood at local distributors or order online at:

- www.systemthree.com: (800) 333-5514
- www.westsystem.com: (866) 937-8797

1 Spread the epoxy, then lightly drag the brush back through to even it out and eliminate bubbles. Work quickly and allow the thick epoxy to flatten without brushing it too much.

NATURAL-BRISTLE BRUSH

EPOXY

2 Sand each coat with 120-grit sandpaper to flatten out any ridges and flaws, then clean and resand with 220-grit to create a smooth, scratch-free surface for the varnish.

UNSANDED EPOXY

3 Apply three coats of oil-based spar varnish with a high-quality china-bristle brush, brushing with the grain. Sand the varnish between coats.

GLOSSY SPAR VARNISH

(100) Apply a bump-free polyurethane finish

This is the best way to apply an oil-based polyurethane varnish. If you choose to use a water-based product, the only difference in application is that you shouldn't thin the water-based varnish to use as a sealer; instead, buy a clear, water-based sealer. The water-based formulas have the advantage of drying faster, so the waiting time is shorter.

First things first

If you've got a rough wood surface, you'll get poor results no matter how meticulous you are about applying the finish. Sand the surface with progressively finer paper until you get to 220-grit. On a newly built table, for example, use a medium (100-grit) sandpaper over the entire surface, then fine (150-grit), then finish with extra-fine (220-grit).

Get all the dust off with a brush and vacuum, then wipe the area with a clean cloth dampened with denatured alcohol. This is a volatile product, so be sure you've got adequate ventilation. Work in a clean environment where you won't kick up dust.

If you want to add color to the wood before varnishing, apply stain or dye according to the manufacturer's instructions. If you use stain, be sure to wipe it evenly after it's had time to soak into the wood. Let the stain dry thoroughly before applying any sealer or finish. For some types of stain, you'll have to wait overnight. After the stain is dry, clean the surface of any dust. Note: To clear up any confusion about the compatibility of polyurethane varnishes and stains, you can use any water-, alcohol- or oil-based stain and then use either a water-based or oil-based polyurethane as a topcoat.

Sealing the surface: the first coat

A clear sealer is like a primer that soaks into the wood surface. It allows the varnish to flow more evenly and adhere better to the workpiece.

Some stains are self-sealing (it'll say so on the can), meaning they have a sealer built into them. If you're using this type of stain, move on to "The Second Coat."

If you're using a stain without a built-in sealer, a dye, or are just leaving your wood natural, you have two choices. You can buy a clear sealer, or make a thinned mixture of three parts oil-based polyurethane and two parts mineral spirits.

Buy a good natural-bristle brush for applying the oil-based sealer. Make sure the surface is dust-free, then brush the sealer on evenly using long strokes (Photo 1). Apply only enough sealer to cover the surface without leaving dry spots. Catch any drips along the edges with your brush before the sealer dries.

The second coat

Now you'll use the polyurethane right out of the can. Load your brush (use a synthetic-bristle brush for water-based polyurethane and a natural-bristle for oil-based) without wiping it along the rim of the can. This will help prevent air

1 Brush oil-based sealer on with a natural-bristle brush. Spread the sealer evenly across the previously stained surface, making sure to catch any runs.

2 Use undiluted polyurethane varnish right out of the can for the second and third coats. After you have it spread evenly, make long, overlapping brush strokes with the grain.

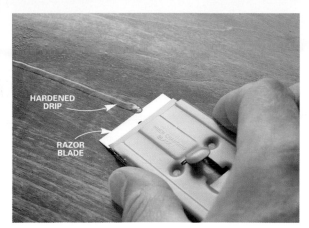

3 Cut away any drips with a razor blade after each coat has dried. Be sure not to cut into the surrounding finish. Small drips will disappear when you wet-sand the finish.

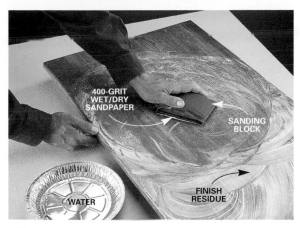

4 Wet-sand the varnish after the second and third coats to remove any blemishes or dust particles. Don't be too aggressive or you'll sand through the finish.

bubbles in the brushed-on varnish. Spread the varnish over the entire surface with long, even strokes. Don't use too much varnish because you're more likely to get runs; brush on just enough to cover the surface evenly.

As soon as the surface is coated, brush over it once again in the direction of the grain from end to end (Photo 2). Overlap your strokes to get the varnish uniform. Now is the time to catch any drips that might appear, especially along the edges. Let this coat dry for about 24 hours.

Fixing imperfections

If you've got any drips from the first two coats, slice them away with a razor blade (Photo 3). Be very careful not to cut through the rest of the finish and into the wood. This step requires steadiness; take your time.

Before you apply the third coat, you're bound to find some other blemishes and dust particles locked into the finish. Now is the time to sand them, along with the edges of any runs you repaired. Use 400-grit wet/dry sandpaper (it's black) mounted on a sanding block (Photo 4). Get the paper wet and sand the surface to remove any bumps of dust or bubbles. Use enough water to lubricate the paper as you sand. You'll know you've got enough water when the paper glides across the surface. As you sand, use light pressure so you don't burn through the surface. Also, be extra careful near the edges where the finish will be thinnest. When the surface feels smooth, wipe it with a damp cloth to remove the sanding residue, then wipe it with a clean, dry cloth.

The third coat and final touch-up

Brush on this coat the same way you applied the second coat and let it dry for 24 hours. If you're lucky, you'll have a smooth, even finish and your work is done. You may, how-

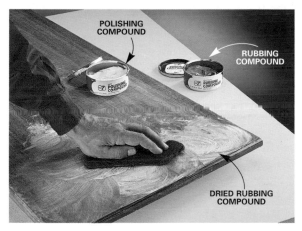

5 Polish the surface if you still have flaws after the third coat has completely dried. Use an automotive rubbing compound first, then polishing compound. Finally, buff the surface with a clean cotton cloth.

ever, have some dust settle into the finish or find another run to fix. If you've got a little fix-up work to do, follow the same procedure as before.

If your third coat still had a few flaws and you had to sand lightly, you'll need to remove the scratches left by the sandpaper. Wait an extra day to let the surface cure. Then use a damp cloth and rub the surface in a circular motion with automotive rubbing compound, available at auto parts stores. The rubbing compound contains fine abrasives, so use it sparingly.

Next, go to a finer-grit compound (Photo 5) called "polishing compound." This will remove the fine scratches left by the rubbing compound. Then buff the surface with a clean cotton cloth until it shines. If the surface is a bit cloudy, wait a few days for the surface to really harden, then rub in a little Johnson's paste wax, available at hardware stores, and hand-buff the surface to achieve a fine luster.

101 Drilling
through hard stuff

Making holes in soft materials like wood is easy. You just stick a standard drill bit in your drill and pull the trigger. But use this approach on harder materials like metal, masonry, glass or tile, and you'll waste time, ruin drill bits and even wreck your workpiece.

Here you'll learn how to choose the right bits and techniques for making holes in hard materials.

Drilling into glass

Drilling a hole in a pane of glass or a mirror is simple. The key is to use a carbide bit made especially for glass and tile (photos above and right). You'll find these bits at most home centers alongside other drill bits or ceramic tile tools. They cost from $5 to $10, depending on size.

Because glass is extremely smooth and hard, the bit will want to wander as you start drilling. To give the bit a foothold, tape a small scrap of dense cardboard (like cereal box cardboard) to the glass. Begin at very low rpm to create a dimple in the glass, then remove the cardboard and continue at about 400 rpm. If you're drilling on a horizontal surface, you can pour a little oil on the area. Make sure the glass is firmly supported on the back side and place only very light pressure on the drill; press too hard and you'll crack the glass. The bit creates a clean hole on the side it enters, but usually chips the edges of the hole on the other side. Note: You can't drill tempered glass.

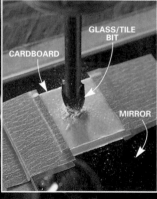

GLASS/TILE BIT

CARDBOARD

MIRROR

Drilling into metal

Most of the drill bits you use for wood will also bore into metal. But a spinning drill bit tends to wander across metal's hard, smooth surface before it begins to dig in. You can give the bit an exact starting point using a center punch and a hammer. The punch creates a tiny dimple that keeps the bit in place (photo, right). With a soft metal like aluminum, you can use a nail instead of a punch.

A little oil helps you drill faster and keeps the bit cooler, so it stays sharp longer. There are special drilling oils, but you can use just about anything—motor oil, transmission fluid, kerosene, even cooking oil. On a slanted surface, keep the oil in place with a ring of plumber's putty, glazing compound or even Play-Doh.

If you're drilling holes larger than 1/4 in. through metal more than 1/16 in. thick, save time by boring smaller pilot holes first. The tips of many drill bits have a flat spot that doesn't slice into metal nearly as well as the sharp outer "lips." By first drilling a pilot hole with a small bit—about the same diameter as the flat spot on the larger bit—you allow the larger bit to cut faster. Seal the underside of the hole with duct tape to keep oil from draining away.

Use firm, steady pressure and moderate speed (600 to 700 rpm) until you're nearly done. As the bit breaks through the other side of the metal, the lips can grab the thin remaining edges. This causes the workpiece (or drill) to spin and might leave you with a broken drill bit or workpiece or even injuries. You can avoid all of this if you ease off the pressure and go to full drill speed just before breakthrough. To be on the safe side, always clamp workpieces in place.

CENTER PUNCH

OIL

DIMPLE

GLAZING COMPOUND

FLAT SPOT

LIP

Getting the speed right

Running your drill too fast can cause heat buildup and ruin drill bits. Drill speed is measured in rpm (revolutions per minute). On the side of any variable-speed drill, you'll find a sticker that lists the rpm range: "0 to 2,000 rpm," for example.

Drills don't have exact settings or speedometers, so you can't run one precisely at the speed you want. But if you know your drill's maximum speed, you can come close enough by the sound of the motor and the feel of the trigger. Squeeze the trigger slowly and gradually increase to full speed. Then gradually decrease speed. Do this a couple of times and you'll develop a feel for where the trigger produces half-speed or quarter-speed and what those speeds sound like. This is easier with cordless drills, since most have high and low ranges.

Drilling into ceramic tile

Tile varies greatly in hardness. You can drill some types of tile using a standard carbide masonry bit. Harder tile requires the bit you'd use for glass. In either hard or soft tile, you can make a hole large enough for plumbing fixtures with a carbide grit hole saw (photo, below), which costs about $16 at home centers and tile suppliers.

To get a hole started without wandering, use the cardboard trick shown on p. 142. The hole saw works best at low speeds (100 to 200 rpm). It cuts slowly and creates a lot of heat, sometimes enough to crack the tile. To prevent "heat shock," immerse the tile in a shallow pool of water. Water keeps everything cool and actually helps the hole saw cut a little faster. Place a scrap of plywood under the tile so you don't drill through the pan.

HOLE SAW

TILE

PLYWOOD SCRAP

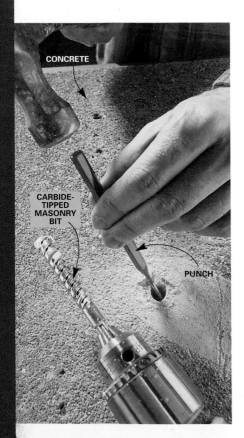

CARBIDE GRIT

HOLE SAW

CAUTION:
Water and electricity are a dangerous combination. Plug your drill into a GFCI-protected outlet or use a cordless drill.

Drilling into masonry

Most forms of masonry—mortar, stucco, brick and concrete block—are fairly easy to drill. Use a carbide-tipped masonry bit (photo, left), push hard and run your drill at about 1,000 rpm. Pull the bit out of the hole occasionally to clear out the powder created by drilling. To make drilling a large hole easier, begin with a small bit and work up: 1/4 in. to 3/8 in. to 1/2 in., for example.

When you're using a standard drill, concrete presents problems that other types of masonry don't because it's full of small stones. Some of these stones are soft enough to drill through easily. But if you hit a hard one, it will stop your progress dead. When you hit a hard stone, keep drilling for a few seconds— you might break through. If not, simply move over and try another spot. If the hole has to be precisely placed, use a punch or small chisel to break up the stone.

A standard corded or cordless drill is fine for drilling a couple of holes in masonry. But if you have to make lots of holes, use a hammer drill to speed up the job (bottom photo). Hammer drills not only spin the bit but also hammer it forward thousands of times per minute. Hammer drill prices begin at about $80. Or you can rent one for $10 to $15 per day.

CONCRETE

CARBIDE-TIPPED MASONRY BIT

PUNCH

HAMMER DRILL

B 6600